D0722319

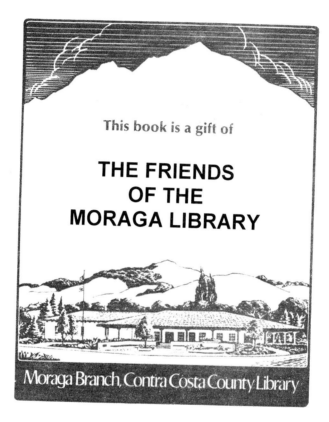

MY UNSPOKEN TRUTH NOW TOLD

MY UNSPOKEN
TRUTH
NOW TOLD

ABIGAIL COUZENS

Charleston, SC
www.PalmettoPublishing.com

My Unspoken Truth Now Told

Copyright © 2020 by Abigail Couzens

First Edition

Hardcover ISBN: 978-1-64990-483-6

Paperback ISBN: 978-1-64111-741-8

eBook ISBN: 978-1-64111-917-7

CONTENTS

DEDICATION

I AM SO overwhelmed and honored to have been trusted with this assignment. I give my Lord and Savior all the credit for teaching me just how to tell my story. I also give thanks and honor to my Spiritual Mother, Dr. Cindy Trimm. Late-night calls, early-morning text messages—you were there. Momma Trimm your encouragement and guidance in completing this project is much appreciated. I literally could not have done this without you.

With extreme gratitude I am blessed for the great insight of my upbringing from my mother, Carmen Santiago, and father, Hiram Gonzalez. Because of my parents' excitement for me writing this book, our conversations were light. And those heavy experiences that could have been hard to discuss were the most peaceful and truthful topics. I also could not have written this book without my siblings. I had many tearful days with them on the phone but even through my tears, I was encouraged, prayed over, and given the strength to write one chapter then another chapter, until it was all put together. To my sisters, Sandra Gonzalez, Carmen Gonzalez, Elisa Brown, Rebecca Baylis, and to my brother Hiram Gonzalez Jr.—thank you. Thank you for your great insight and motivation. Noemi, I want to say thank you for always being there and giving me your thoughts and input when asked for and needed.

Moneshia, we could talk and cry about this for hours, but you would not let me. Thank you for being the best friend I needed back in 2004, when I felt I could not press on. To my FRAN, Pastor Mya Miller, who knows the true meaning of fasting and praying. At any moment, I knew I could call on you, Pastor Miller, and go into fasting and praying concerning this project. I appreciate you, Pastor Miller, for checking in and making sure I was on task with my writhing. I am forever grateful for our friendship and sisterhood. Last but not least, I am so humble to honor my husband, Bishop Dr. Victor S. Couzens. Thank you, baby, for wiping my eyes every time I was done writing for the day. Thank you for sacrificing the home office and computer just so I could write. Those nights when I felt the inspiration to write and you needed to prepare or go over your sermon notes, you allowed me the office while you patiently sat on the couch and began working on your cell phone. I am forever grateful. I could not have asked for a better partner or companion. You are and have been a tremendous blessing to me. I love you, dear. Thank you to many who have kept me in your prayers. I pray you find that your prayers have not been in vain once you read this book. I thank you and love you all.

-Abigail Couzens

INTRODUCTION

YES! THAT TOUCH right there. The way your fingers run through my body. The way you penetrate. Slowly. In and out. In and out. I scream, but it just motivates you. Tears running down my face, but you find it more fulfilling. My body so tight. I wasn't used to anything like this before. But, how could I be? I was only seven. But that did not stop you. Eight, nine, ten. Here I am, thinking, *When will this stop?*

~Damaged

I never fell in love with the idea of sex. Rather, I got comfortable with that piece of darkness. I carried it year after year. I did not love him. It was just the energy between my legs that brought on the chemistry. But what did I have to offer? Nothing. How old was I? I'm losing count. Wait, that's right. I was eleven now. Where was my father? How much longer did he have in prison? I knew that, when he came out, he would protect me from this mess of a life. Twelve, thirteen—then it happened.

I yelled, "Daddy, you're home! I'm so happy to see you."

Before I could say another word, my father looked at me and said, "I know."

I stood there frozen. I did not know what to say or if I should say anything at all. So I waited. Waited some more. Then finally my daddy spoke.

He said in a low sweet voice, "I know you've been touched, but I promise you, I'm home now. No one, and I mean no one, will ever touch you like that again."

I rested my head on my daddy's shoulders and cried. All I could say was, "Welcome home, Daddy. Welcome home!"

While this introduction might seem intense, it's a sneak peek into *My Unspoken Truth Now Told*. I don't regret these events; they have built me into the woman that I am today—strong, powerful, loyal, and mature. The actions taken throughout this book are not being told to garner sympathy, but so that someone, some child who may be in my shoes, could know that there is hope. You do have a choice. You do not have to live your life being sexually abused. It is not your fault, and there is always help available. Suicide is not the answer. Cutting your wrist won't stop the pain, but it will cause more agony. There's no pill or drink that could drown these experiences away. The only solution is to tell someone. And trust and believe that there is a God and that He has the whole world in his hands.

CHAPTER 1
THE BIRTH

FEBRUARY 21, 1986—THE day my existence had a purpose. The day God believed the forming in my mother's womb was enough; it was now time for my mother to thrust. February 21, 1986 was the date I was conceived. Or was it the date I would always regret? I was born and raised in North Philly, with four other siblings in the house. I had one brother and three sisters with the same mother. We all lived in a three-bedroom house. You may be wondering how that worked. Well, of course, my mother had her own room. My brother, being the only boy, had his own room. And, yes, there were three girls in one room with two sets of bunk beds. I was just a baby, so I'm assuming I was in my mother's room.

Let me fast forward to when I was about nine months old. It was a nice cool day, as my mother tells me, when suddenly one of my sisters heard this loud rumbling noise. It sounded as if I had fallen down the steps. And that's exactly what had happened. Right at that moment, when my sister heard the rumbling noise, everything stopped. It was I, falling down the basement steps.

"Abigail!" my sister shouted.

But was it too late? Did she get to me in time? My mother, who had been cooking in the kitchen, now rushed over to the basement steps. In my baby walker, I had rolled down the entire flight of stairs leading to the basement. One step, two steps, ten steps down. Yikes! Who left the basement door open? My mother rushed down the basement steps, but to her surprise, I was smiling. I was laughing. Both my mother and sister were now amazed and yet confused about what had just happened. This was impossible. For me to be smiling and laughing after a hard fall at nine months old it seemed impossible. In total amazement, my mother was left to believe it must have been an angel. It was at that moment that my mother knew there was something special about me. Although many had been telling my mother that her pregnancy would be a blessing, their words had never rung true in my mother's ears. But we'll get to that a little later. My mother checked me from head to toe, but there wasn't one scratch. Just me, sitting at the bottom of the steps, while my walker stood against the wall. There I was, ten steps down, as if nothing had ever happened. You tell me: how was that possible? What did this mean for my life?

Will I fall down plenty of steps in life and still find myself smiling and laughing at the end? Does this indicate that death will continue to chase me from this moment forward, since death has been chasing me from my mother's womb? You may be wondering how death has been chasing me from my mother's womb. The simple answer is this: "I was a mistake." Not in my own eyes; not in the eyes of God—but I was considered a mistake to just one parent. To the other parent, I was considered more like a miracle. And because of those differences in my parent's opinions of me, I was raised feeling like a mistake to one and a miracle to another. It's not surprising to me that this fall occurred but no harm prospered. It takes me back to the scripture that states, "No weapons formed against you shall prosper" (Isaiah 54:17, NKJV).

I stand here today, believing that, at the age of nine months, it was the hand of God that protected and covered me. God knew I had to be saved as a child because my purpose would be greater than this fall. And since death had already taken place on my behalf by the King of Kings and Lord of Lords, Christ figured it would be too soon for me to go. So He kept me. Every tumble, every step I fell down, His arms was there to carry me through. I may have fallen then, but I stand here today with all victory in my hands. And no devil in hell will ever be able to move, shake, or break me. I am not a mistake. I am here on purpose with a purpose. And because I am aware of that, I am now a threat to the enemy. He's been trying to kill me for a long time. But touch not Gods anointed. I write to you today to encourage you. The enemy is trying to kill something in you, and this is an indication that what you are carrying is powerful. And he knows, if he can get you to abort your mission, then he wins. Remind him that greater is He that is you than he that is in the world "(1 John 4:4 KJV)." Your presence is no accident or mistake. Your presence is a weapon.

The next day after my fall down the basement steps, I was in the living-room floor playing with my toys, and the doorbell rang. Or at least, my father thought he heard the doorbell. He walked toward the door, and as he got closer, he saw what he thought had to be my hand playing in the mail slot.

"Abigail!" he shouted, "get away from the door!"

He was sure that it was I. It was my hand, my face, and my clothes. But as he got closer, he noticed it was not. I was still sitting in the living-room floor, playing with my toys. At that moment my, father saw something: a white shadow, like an image of a hand. As my father opened the door, he saw that no one stood there. The shadow had quickly vanished. He swiftly picked me up and said,

"The hand of God is on you, child, and the image that I saw looked just like you." I did not understand him then. I just smiled and wanted to play with Daddy. But looking back now, I can see how the hand of the Almighty was on me. I mean, just a day before, those same Holy hands had saved me when I rolled down the basement steps in my baby walker. The hand of God was over me heavily as a child.

My father sat me down, and I continued to play with my toys. He rested himself on the couch as he tried to understand what had just happened. Here he was trying to understand what all of this meant for me. After a while, he continued on with his day. I was only nine months old, and this proved to be the second indication that God's hand was truly over my life. And while I may have fallen on numerous occasions in my lifetime, I've always been held up. There were times that I experienced the pain of the fall, but God has always showed me why the pain was necessary. I don't regret any of falls that I've encountered; because of them, I have a book today.

———

Let's skip ahead a few years so I can show you who I was through the age of three. I remember always wanting to play with BB guns, water guns—anything that had to do with a gun. My interest in being a police officer started at a really young age. I remember playing cops and robbers all by myself. I would run, and then I would catch myself. It's OK to laugh. I would run then quickly turn around and tell myself to freeze. I would actually freeze. Then I would serve myself my rights. It sounded something like this:

"You are under arrest. You have the right to be quiet and find help. You have the right to call Mommy and Daddy. You have the right to bring one toy to jail, because that's where you're going buddy."

I am fully aware now that those were not the correct words to use. But hey, no one corrected me. So, I picked up one doll baby, and to jail I went. I used to sit in the corner alone, waiting for someone to get me out. Instead, I would hear, "Get up and out of the corner," my sister Elisa would yell. That was good enough for me. I took that as me being set free.

EXCERPTS FROM MY PERSONAL JOURNAL

Starting this entry today is a bit emotional. I really tried to think of just about everything I could to figure out why I am being treated so differently than the rest. My siblings seem to receive more attention from my mother than I do. Now granted, none of us equally gets affection, but this lack of attention is really starting to bother me. Could it be that the pieces of my own puzzle are starting to connect and are beginning to show me just who is the parent that considers me a miracle and who counts me a mistake. The way my pieces are forming together, it's showing that I am my mother's mistake and my father's miracle. But why?

What have I done so wrong to deserve this different type of treatment? I'm starting to believe maybe that's why the basement door was left open. No, stop. You're going too far, Abby. But really, why else would the basement door be open? And to this day, no one can give a reason why the door was unlocked and open. The pieces of my life's puzzle don't seem fair, but I guess it's time to live up to the hand that life has dealt me. I wonder if I'll ever get to have this conversation with my mother. Maybe when I'm older—she wouldn't mind explaining to me just what exactly happened. All I know is that I am no mistake. I was purposely formed in my mother's womb. I was thought of before my mother and father ever met each another. If you are struggling with your existence, if you've ever been told that you are a mistake, this letter is for you, as it is for me.

WE ARE NOT A MISTAKE! GOD LOVES US AND WE SHALL PROVE TO THE WORLD THAT THEY SHOULD HAVE NEVER COUNTED US OUT.

A note to all parents: it's never fair to show favoritism among your children. Consider the damage being done when one child is constantly feeling left out. Why not seek help or counsel? So often I hear parents say how their child needs therapy. And while I have strong feelings about that, have you ever considered we may need therapy because of you? Because of how you treated and abandoned us. Let us dig into the real issues of life. Let us stop living our lives as if everything is in-tact when, in all reality, nothing is together. If this is the hand I've been given, then sit and watch me play it. But I refuse to feel like a mistake. I'll live life to the fullest. And one day I'll prove, once and for all, that having me was and is a blessing.

CHAPTER 2
THE ADDITION

FEBRUARY 21, 1991. I was five years old now, and my mother's stomach had enlarged. I wasn't too sure what was happening. All I knew was that there was no birthday party set-up for me this day. No cake, no ice cream, no gifts, nothing. Just my older female siblings yelling, "Let it be a girl!" and my only brother yelling, "Let it be a boy!" But it was my birthday. I was trying to understand why we were chanting for another female or male when I was standing right here. Maybe they'd all forgotten it was my birthday. What could be more exciting than me turning five? I mean, my siblings were at it for a while. The chant went on and on. And since this day was a total waste, I would rather find out what the whole commotion was all about.

Then I was told that our mother was in labor and was going to be having a baby. Well now, that explained what the chanting was all about. So now I was excited, and I wanted to join in on the chant. I joined my sisters in shouting, "Let it be a girl!"

I was only able to do that for about thirty minutes before I got tired. Want to hear something funny? All of that chanting and no baby. False alarm. It wasn't until seven days later that we got the call from the hospital. The call we'd all been waiting for. Was it a girl, or was it a boy? We were all so overwhelmed. Then it happened; we heard, "It's a girl!"

My sisters and I were so excited. My brother wasn't as thrilled. He wanted a younger brother. This was the fifth girl from my mother. And he was still the only boy. Mom was coming home that day with the baby. Everyone was getting prepared to meet this new kid on the block. The room was ready. Teddy bears were laid out. We were all eagerly awaiting the arrival. Then my sister yelled out, "She's here!" Wow. I was no longer the baby. I now had a baby sister, and her name was Rebecca.

————

It was Sunday morning; rise and shine. Church was mandatory in this house. We were never late to church. My mother was able to get all six kids up and ready and on time for church. Well, truth be told, it didn't take much to be on time. Church was happening in our basement. That's right. Monday through Saturday, our basement was a playroom, but on Sundays, it was the sanctuary. The pastor was amazing. Even though I was young at the time, I can remember everything about this pastor. He was sharp. Although he preached in Spanish and I barely understood what he said, it didn't matter. I just enjoyed watching him. He was my hero. He was my daddy. Like literally, my biological father was the pastor. And here is a twist for you: although I enjoyed watching my daddy preach and do his thing, I absolutely dreaded going down there. Sunday after Sunday, as quick as it came—that's how fast I wanted it to be over. I had one small yet major problem. Why was he looking at me so strangely? Why did he just stare at me? *Oh gosh here he comes. Don't look, don't look. Just sit tight.*

"Hello," he said.

I stayed silent.

He continued with "Your mother is busy with the baby; your dad is preaching. Do you want me to sit with you?"

"No," I quickly answered.

I wish I'd known about social distancing back then. But I was six now, so of course, he did not listen. He took a seat next to me. Ugh. He wasn't the smallest man on the planet, if you know what I mean. Clothes were too tight. He took up two chairs. And he forced himself to fit next to me. Unbelievable. Was he not aware of himself? Why was he so close? Why was nobody saying anything to him?

I thank God for the snappy attitude I had even as a kid.

"Excuse me, mister. Move your hand."

I'm not sure why he felt the need to place his oversized hand on my baby knee. I guessed he was shocked at my request for him to remove his hand. He quickly asked that I lower my voice and be quiet.

Instead I said, "I could get louder if you like."

So, he got up and moved.

"Good," I whispered. "And don't come back."

Although my attitude was a little snappy, I still sat there shaking. I wasn't sure if I'd been disrespectful or if I had done the right thing. My thoughts raced: *Do I tell momma? No. She's busy with the baby. Do I tell Daddy? No. I will just keep it to myself. It won't happen again.* At least, that's what I thought. But he didn't stop. Sunday after Sunday, he insisted on sitting next to me and placing his oversized hand on my baby knee. And each week, I had to remind him to move it. Why did I even have to deal with this at six years old? Was no one else seeing this? A church full of people, and *no one* saw this man wanting to sit next to me every Sunday? I don't get it.

One particular Sunday, my mother was teaching Sunday school. So, I went to join in on the class. Lucky me. My job was to keep an eye on my little baby sister, so I didn't have to take the exam that was given to the bigger kids on that day. I remember this Sunday school class being one of a kind. The exam was given. My mother specifically announced, "Read each question before starting." No one listened. But boy oh boy, by the time they all got to the final question on the exam, they all wished they had read each question. The last question stated, "Now that you have read each question just turn in your exam. You do not need to answer any of the fifteen questions." It was hilarious. My sister Elisa called it "the art of following directions."

Sunday school was over, so it was time to prepare for the worship service. My mother asked me to stay with the baby while she went and warmed up her milk. I was glad to do so. While my mother was going up the steps to warm up the milk, can you guess who was coming down? Yes, the big guy with the oversized hand.

"Hola, Abby," he said.

I completely ignored him, but then he asked to hold the baby. Let me tell you all how fast I said, "No! Absolutely not! You can't hold my baby sister."

With my snappy mouth, I shared that she was hungry and I was waiting for the milk to feed her. That didn't sit too well with him. In an unfriendly tone, he demanded, "Give me the baby. I am her godfather."

I stared. Godfather? What did that mean? Did that mean he would be in her life forever? Would he try to touch her baby knee too? I was so confused. Yet at six years old, I held my ground.

I said again, "No. My mother is now returning and coming down the steps with the milk." It felt like it was taking her forever to get down the steps that day. I reached for the milk. My mother popped my hand. The man started small-talking my mother. He started to say how big the baby was getting—blah, blah, blah, blah, blah. He turned around and gave me a smirk. My mother asked him if he wanted to hold the baby. *For goodness sake! Just give me the milk*, was all I was thinking. The last thing I wanted him to ever do was hold my baby sister. *Think fast, think fast, think fast.* I quickly pinched my little sister to make her cry. Hey, don't judge me. It worked.

I quickly said, "No, Mom, don't let him hold her; she's crying now. She's hungry. Let me give her the bottle."

Surprisingly, my mother agreed. She gave me the bottle. I fed my sister and whispered in her tiny little ear, "I'm sorry, but it was for your own good." From that moment onward, I was determined to never allow him to get close to my little sister. I thought, if I just pinched her every time he was around, that would work. But that didn't always work. After all, he was her godfather, and I was only six years old. The times he did pick her up, oh believe me, I had radar eyes on him. Each time he checked out ok but I guess he had to with me always being smack dead in his face with an attitude of an eighteen-year-old.

———

The entire house was in a panic. Mother was hollering for us to call the ambulance. My father was lying still on the couch, spasming every few minutes. I had questions. I wanted to know exactly what was happening to my daddy. Things got worse when his entire body started shaking uncontrollably. I just wanted him to stop. Tears rushing down my face, I shouted, "Papi [a Spanish word for dad] please what's wrong?"

A few minutes later, the ambulance arrived, and they took my father. I was not able to go to the hospital where they were taking him. So I stayed home with my siblings. Soon, we were all informed that my father had a stroke. I wasn't aware of the seriousness of a stroke. I was just a kid. All I wanted to know was whether he was alive. I was informed that Daddy was alive and would be OK and that a stroke was normal for people to have. And again, using my typical 100 questions I wanted to know the type of person this was "normal" for. Was there a certain lifestyle my daddy had that I should be aware of? Was there something he smoked or drank that I should stay away from? But those questions didn't make sense to ask, because my father didn't smoke or drank. Later, I found out that my father was dealing with a heart condition that could have possibly caused the stroke. Doctors tried to say my daddy had a weak heart and they was not sure how much longer he would have to live. That was devastating to hear. I needed my daddy. I was a daddy's girl, and that was the worst thing ever told to me.

I gladly write this book not when I'm six years old but when I'm 34 years old, and I'm happy to report that my father is still alive today. He is still dealing with a weak heart, but he is alive and well. After my father had been on bed rest for a while, he was finally back up and at it. He was preaching again but, this time, at a different location. Service was no longer in our basement. It was now down the street and around the corner. We moved the service from our basement to a local building on Ninth and Lehigh. Services were still being held in Spanish. I asked a random church member about having an English service. She looked at me and laughed. To this day, I'm trying to find out what was so funny. She never did answer.

Now, as I think about it, I wonder if she even knew English. I guess I'll never know. While we had our church services in this new building, something strange was taking place among my siblings. They began making weird hand gestures with their fingers. And to my surprise, they understood one another. I asked one of my siblings what exactly they were doing. And she said, "Sign language." Sign language? What was that? It was a way to communicate, since we couldn't talk in church. Oh, I was impressed. By using sign language, they talked all throughout the service.

EXCERPTS FROM MY PERSONAL JOURNAL

I think I'm too young to be feeling like this. I don't get it. Daddy doesn't touch my knee like this. Daddy doesn't slide his hand up in between my thighs. Why does this big guy get to do it? I know people see him doing it because the lady next to me at church seen him and when I turned my head for help, she quickly turned the other way. I don't understand how there is a room full of people and I seem to be the only one being touched. I hate him. Why does he come Sunday after Sunday to just bother me? What do I have that others don't have? Why couldn't he find another church to attend on Sundays? One day I'm going to tell Daddy. I'm going to tell him everything. I just want him to stop touching me. And he better not ever touch my baby sister. I don't have time for this. I don't know where my crayons are. I had them yesterday, and boom, today they are gone. Oh, and since I didn't have a birthday, I would like a bike to make it up. No, I don't know how to ride a bike, but I can learn once I get the bike. Well, I wrote it down. Now the only thing I have to do is ask. Yeah right. There goes my bike. I'll never ask.

CHAPTER 3
THE TAKEAWAY

LET'S GET INTO something a little more interesting. Watching Daddy from the basement steps, I hesitated before I said anything to him. I was trying to figure it out for myself.

"Daddy, what are you doing?"

In shock, he turned around and said, "Nothing. Go back upstairs."

But clearly that "nothing" was actually something. Being who I was, I didn't ask any more questions. I just looked and listened. I mean, he was just in the basement, carving dices. Yes. You read it right—he was downstairs in the basement, with a knife in one hand, carving dices. About forty minutes later, he came upstairs.

My mother demanded he go to the store for milk, bread, and eggs. I remember because he asked me to hold the food stamps. Aye, food stamps—you know, the money that came in the book? The one you had to rip out every time you wanted to use a dollar? Good ole days.

So here we went, Daddy and me, to the store to buy milk, bread, and eggs.

Suddenly, Daddy said, "Wait right here."

I stood back as he shouted to some guys, "I'm in!"

They seemed to all know my daddy.

"What's up, OG?" someone stated.

"Hey, little Abby!" someone else shouted.

I just stood there on the corner of Thirteenth and York, waiting for Daddy to finish. He rolled once, he rolled twice, and he rolled three times. He was winning. It was his lucky day. Or maybe they were some lucky dice he was playing with. Maybe we could save the food stamps Mom gave us and use the money he was winning. He won again. This time, someone yelled, "Hold on OG. Let me see them dice." My dad got up, grabbed his dice, and put his hands in his pocket. "No, no, no, OG. Get your hands out of your pocket. Show us them dice you was just rolling with."

I got nervous. This was something you thought you would only see on TV.

"Go home little Abby."

Huh? I was being told to go home? One of the guys surrounding my daddy said, "Go home little Abby. Walk down York Street back to Eleventh Street."

"I'm not going nowhere without my dad," I yelled back.

One said, "This is not the time little, Ab. Go back down Eleventh Street."

I looked at my daddy. He looked at me. He said, "Go. Go home. Run home."

I shouted back, "Mom said we have to buy, milk, bread, and eggs."

He said again, "Go home Abigail."

I ran and I cried. Why wasn't my daddy coming back home with me? What had happened? Everyone was just cheering and having what seemed to be a good time. How did it lead to this? I did not go straight home. I ran to another corner store across the playground.

I brought momma the milk, bread, and eggs that she had asked for. It was heavy, I must add, and I was out of breath. Momma, with a disgusted look on her face, asked me about my father. She wanted to know where he had stopped. I had no idea what to say at this point. I'm a protector, so I lied. I told my momma he was with some friends. I guess my momma knew better. With that same sickened look, she responded, "That is a lie, Abigail."

I didn't know what to say after her response. After all, it was a lie. I put the milk, bread, and eggs away and just sat by the living-room window.

I waited. And I waited. I waited all day for Daddy to come home. I told nobody. I kept what had just happened to myself. Daddy didn't come home that night. So, the next day, I could not wait to walk to school. Hartranft Elementary School was the place to be. But this day, it seemed so far away. It was the longest four blocks I'd ever walked. When I got there, I rushed up to one of my good friends. I knew she had a big brother, like the guys who'd surrounded my daddy. I asked her if it would be ok if I spoke with her brother. She assured me it was no problem. After school I ran up to my friend's brother, I'll call him Neal. "Neal," I shouted.

In shock he said, "Yes?"

I quickly said, "Some guys have my daddy. He was rolling the dice, then suddenly it got serious. I was told to run home, but Daddy didn't come with me. So then I went to the corner store across the park, and then…"

"Slow down; slow down." Neal stopped me. He began to ask me questions. My voice began to crack. I fought to keep my tears back.

"What street were you on?"

"We were on Thirteenth and York Neal."

"OK, listen," Neal said, "everybody knows your old man. That's OG. I'll get some of my guys from Ninth and Huntington. And we'll make a trip to Thirteenth and York."

"OK, Neal. Thank you so much."

The guys on 9th and Huntington were just as tough as the guys from 13th street. I wasn't sure how this was going to turn out, but none of that concerned me. The only thing I was concerned with was finding out where my daddy was. I left the presence of Neal and did not say another word to anybody. Around 6:00 p.m., I heard sirens. I peeked outside to see where they were coming from. I was not surprised to find them heading to 13th and York, where my daddy had been playing street dice. Was he dead? Did they kill him? My heart was racing. I was too young for this. This was too much pressure. But I still said nothing. I'd learned at an early age how to bottle up issues and to seal them with a tight cap. These lessons have truly been playing a part even in my adult life. It's the reason I can hold a lot in—but when the cap goes flying off, I am a complete mess. There has to be an easier way to deal with all that I'm holding inside. Little by little, I am learning how to express my feelings. I can honestly say having that release makes a world of difference.

I saw Neal the next day.

"Your OG is good."

"What? But where is he? Where is he, Neal, and did you see him for yourself?"

All Neal said was, "The message back to you, little mama, is that he's OK. He'll be back soon."

"Wait. What? He's OK; he'll be back soon? That's it?"

Soon seemed like a lifetime. Where was my daddy? Where had they taken him? I had so many questions and no one to answer them. Each day, I waited for Daddy, but he never returned. I started to keep track of the days, but after forty-five days, I gave up. I started a journal, and it helped me to release my anger. Almost every day, I would go in our basement and just lay on the floor and cry. I cried for forty-five days, but nothing happened. Daddy still wasn't back. I noticed a small Bible in the basement. I picked it up. Luckily it was in English. Not trying to go to any specific scripture, I opened it up to Joshua 1:5, which states, "I will not leave you or forsake you."

That scripture took me out. It was the first day I cried out loud. I couldn't hold it in any longer. I spoke back to that verse—well, more like screamed back at the verse. I said, "If you'd never leave me or forsake me, then *where* are you? Where is my father? Why hasn't he returned? How am I to function? It's been forty-five days, and I have not told any of my siblings what happened. This is developing a character in me that I don't desire. I don't want to be mean; I don't want to hurt, but this is too overwhelming. How much longer before my father returns?"

I lay on the basement floor until I could get myself together. My face was red, I could tell. I could feel it getting warm minute by minute. My eyes were puffy. I was a complete mess. We had a sink down in our basement, so I patted my face with warm water, lean over the sink and tell myself, "I got this. I got this. I got this." Deep down, I was falling apart. But for some reason, I forced myself to hold it all together. That was fine if that was what I had to do. As a kid, I loved skating. As a matter of fact, all of my mother's children loved skating. I'd watched my older siblings skate, and I was able to pick up some moves. I had some skates in the basement; I would put them on, clear a straight path, and skate back and forth. No one came looking for me; I assumed they could hear my skates. So I was left alone for a few hours. Which was perfect for me. I took this time to practice skating backward. To this day, I absolutely love skating. And I still use skating as a stress reliever.

After a few hours in the basement, my mother called for me. I answered her and made my way up. Wow! It was time for dinner. Time had truly flown by. Sitting at the table, I was quiet for the most part. I honestly can't recall a dinner conversation I've had as a child. I would just sit there and eat. No one asked what was wrong, which was fine with me, because I'd learned to sit there with a straight face so no one could tell that anything was wrong. After dinner, I would help clean up, then I would wash up and just lay down with a book in my hand. I absolutely loved reading as a child. It doesn't surprise me that I am now writing a book of my own.

EXCERPTS FROM MY PERSONAL JOURNAL

I cannot cry anymore. My eyes are beginning to physically hurt when tears begin to well up. I actually have to think happy thoughts just to keep my eyes from hurting. If there is one thing I've learned, it's to never take anyone for granted. I miss my daddy so much. I didn't think it would be over forty-five days before I would be seeing him again. To know that he's OK but I can't see him is nerve wrecking, and it doesn't make any sense. The only thing I can come up with is either he's in jail (but how would Neal know that?) or the guys from Thirteenth and York have taken him, and he's in their safe house.

Everybody knows drug dealers in Philly have a safe house. A safe house is where no one would ever think to look. I'm so tired of this. People would assume that this would probably weaken an individual, but it has strengthened me in a way. It has given me a tougher attitude and outlook on life. And I'm not even a teenager yet. Can you imagine what life is going to be like once I get to my teenage years or even my adult life? I'm scared to see what will come of it. One day I'm leaning on the Lord, then there are other days where I'm like, "What is happening?" I'm starting to understand who I am. I'm loyal. I'm a protector. But am I also a liar? Does sticking up for my father against my mother make me a liar? I mean. I've lied at least once or twice for my daddy, without him even knowing, but clearly that doesn't make me out to be a liar. It's not who I am and what I want to become.

I am thankful for the streets. I can't imagine being raised anywhere else. I hear the suburbs are quieter than the city, but the suburbs could not have given me this backbone and especially at a young age. I have the mind of a teenager. Sometimes even as an adult. But I'm still a kid having to live ahead of my time.

That's fine, if that's what I have to do. But if that's going to be the case, then I don't want nobody on my case.

CHAPTER 4
WHY IS HE BACK?

IT WAS MONDAY morning, 7:30 a.m., and he was at my house visiting our mother. I wasn't too sure of what is being said, but they exchange a few laughs then I was being called. Mother told me to get my things for school and that he was going to drive me. Now why in the world would he have to drive me to school when my legs had been working this whole time? He hadn't taken me to school any other time. What was the big deal? There was absolutely no reason why he would need to drive me four blocks. Standing now next to my mother, I said under my breath, "No, Mom. I can walk."

She looked down at me and said, "Go get your school things. He's going to take you to school."

I didn't move. All I could think about was his oversized hand on my baby knee, sliding up my thigh. Traumatized. My mother looked at me a second time and said, "Go get your school things. He's going to take you to school."

"OK, Mom."

Regretting ever being alive, I was hoping my father would be outside waiting for me, but he wasn't. Into this man's car I went. I was forced to sit in the front. I was seven years old now, and there went that hand again on my knee. I didn't even move. Humiliated, I sat there, immobile. Breaking the silence and slowly raising his hand, he said, "Whom does this belong to?"

I hopped out of the car so fast, I'm not sure if it actually came to a complete stop. I just jumped out and ran. There was Neal. Should I tell him what had just happened? *No, I better not.* I said nothing to no one. Why in his sick mind did he find it OK to touch me? I was only seven. What did I have to offer? Nothing. Did I mention I was only seven? I remember not being able to function in school that day. I didn't even bother getting my lunch, and I never missed lunch. The school bell rang. School was over. I would just walk this out and give my mind time to process what had happened that morning. No, not again. There he was, pulling up slowly with a disgusting grin on his face. I was left to wonder, *Why is he back? Doesn't he have a wife to pertain to? Surly he has a son. He should be more focus on his son than he is with me.* I walked right past his car. But, of course, that just angered him. He didn't let me get too far; in a low voice, he told me to get in.

I quickly said I could walk and that nothing was wrong with my legs today. Oh yes, I had the attitude of a fifteen-year-old. But can you blame me? At this point, I felt myself developing an attitude like no other. And while people wanted to talk about how "nasty" my attitude was or becoming, maybe they should have switched shoes with me. I would have gladly dropped the hand I was dealt. A child's attitude is often built-up pain that they try to express. Take the time to *listen* to your children. I can't express this enough. After keeping him waiting awhile, he demanded I get in his car. So I got in, and immediately he began to ask me questions, as if he was really interested or concerned with my answer.

"How was school?" he asked.

Giving him one-word answers, I just said, "Good."

"You hungry? We can go to McDonalds," he continued. I gave him a sharp answer, indicating I was not hungry and just wanted to be dropped off at the house. I was not looking forward to spending any extra time with him in the car. But to McDonald's we went. There was his hand. There was his finger. That touch right there. The way his fingers ran through my body. The way he penetrated. Slowly. In and out, in and out. I screamed, but it just motivated him. Tears running down my face, but he found it more fulfilling. My body so tight. I wasn't used to anything like this.

But, how could I be? I was only seven.

"*Stop!*" I shouted.

He laughed. Then he asked, "Whom does that belong to?"

I was so confused.

He said, "Let me help you. Let me help you understand. That belongs to me…"

As he patted what was in between my legs.

"What? Move your hand!" I shouted. "And I don't want McDonald's."

Now I was experiencing a feeling that had never risen up before. *Hatred*. This was bigger than anger. At seven years old, I began to develop hate in my heart. As a matter of fact, it was the beginning of hate toward all men. As we pulled up to the drive-through, I was not surprised that he ordered almost everything off the menu. He took me home, and I ran upstairs. I was now angry with my mother. I had told her that I did not need him picking me up or dropping me off. Why was she not listening? That evening after I got my homework done, I headed to my mother's room. I was determined to tell her directly what was happening to me. Knocking on the door, I asked if she was busy. With her response being no, I walked in and wasted no time.

"Mom, it's about the man. I don't need him taking me to school or dropping me off. I can go around the corner and get my friend, and we can go to school together. She doesn't mind. We are really good friends. He just always touches…"

I wasn't able to finish because my mother interrupted, saying, "Stop it. Let him take you to school, since your father is not here and I am here with the baby. I do not want you walking to school alone."

Again, I continued. I wouldn't be alone; I would go around the corner, and my friend and I would walk together.

"Mom, he touches me."

"Abigail, you're lying, my mother continues, he's helping me, since I'm here alone trying to raise all of you. That's that. Now go."

Oh, now I was frustrated. I was now determined to become the child from hell. Did she not understand I wasn't safe? Now what? What was I supposed to do now? I remember not being able to sleep that night. All I kept hearing over and over in my head was, "Whom does this belong to?"

I woke up for school the next day. I got ready, and I remember running to school. Yeah, I saw him outside. What was he going to do? Chase me? Yeah right. He could not even walk straight. So, I ran all four blocks. This day in school was probably the worst for me. I started so much trouble. I didn't care. I was angry. I remember sitting at lunch with two girls that were arguing. Over what I do not know. One girl was sitting right next to me, and the other girl was across from me. All I recall is the one sitting across from me saying, "Do something, do something." So, I took it upon myself to kick the girl under the lunchroom table. Well, she automatically thought the girl she was arguing with had kicked her. A fight then broke out. I had no care in the world. *If I can be touched at just seven years old, surely you two ladies can fight and be all right.* Man, was I wrong. The one sitting across from me got beat up badly. Even though she'd swung first—she probably should have thought that through. She had a busted lip and a black and blue eye.

Both girls were taken to the office while I went to class. Not long into class, there was a knock on the door. The principal and the girl's mother (the girl with the black and blue eye) had asked my teacher to excuse me from class for questioning. I met them outside of the room and said, "Hello," as if I knew nothing. The child's mother went first. She told me how her daughter had a bruised eye and a busted lip, all of which I was very much aware of. She asked me if I had any idea what had happened, since I'd been sitting at the same table with the girls. I laughed and said I knew nothing. The principal had never known me to be disrespectful, and I noticed his posture shifting as I laughed. He stopped me and demanded that I respect this child's mother. I apologized and assured her I had no idea how it had all happened. I shared how sorry I was about her daughter's eye and lip and asked to be excused and sent back to class. I was dismissed, and as I sat down in my classroom seat, I muttered, "I do not care." That was the start of me going downhill.

After school, I caught up with the girl I was sitting next to at lunch, and we just laughed. I told her how the girl's mom had come to the school and asked me questions. We both just laughed. And yes, I saw "that man" outside of my school that day. But I had no care in the world. I knew he couldn't catch me, so I finished my conversation with my friend, and—guess what?—I took off running home. I know he was heated. But all he could do was drive off and met me at my house. Surprisingly, he didn't. I got home, and he was nowhere in sight. *Good*, I thought to myself. I dodged that bullet.

EXCERPTS FROM MY PERSONAL JOURNAL

Maybe I should join the track team when I get to high school. The way I was running today was amazing. I surprised myself. Man, today was a great day. Let's see. What exactly did I accomplish today? A fight in the lunchroom and an argument at recess. Perfect. Even though I was able to laugh about these two events with friends today, inside I am actually torn. This isn't me. This isn't what I want to do or become. But what else am I to do? I feel like somebody has to pay for what is happening to me. And since my own mother does not believe me, what is there left to do? I did learn a valuable listen today. I learned that my anger and issues could hurt those around me. Because I went to school hurt and angry, it caused a classmate to catch a black eye and a busted lip. The one thing I will never forget is what that girl's mother said to me before I was excused to return back to my classroom. She said, "Are you hurt. Because only hurt people hurt people." I have never heard anything like that before. But the truth was, I was hurt, and it caused someone else to hurt. Maybe I can apologize and make things right. But then I'll have to deal with my mother being called, and I just don't have the energy to deal with her. I'll just brush this one under the rug and learn to be more careful with my anger.

Just because I'm hurting doesn't mean I have to go around hurting others. I will never forget that.

CHAPTER 5
THE TOUCH THAT CHANGED MY LIFE

SHOOT, MOM IS *not home. No one is home. It's too quiet. I'll just pretend one of my siblings is upstairs.* I quickly told him thanks for the ride home and that I was going to do my homework with my sister. When I tried to close the door behind me, he stopped it. He let himself in and locked the door behind him. I tried to rush up the steps, but he told me to stop. He walked through the house, seeing if there was really no one home. He walked through the kitchen, he went down to the basement (I should have locked him down there), and then he went upstairs and told me to follow. *If only I could trip and make him fall down the steps,* was really all I was thinking about.

Once upstairs, he checked every room, besides my mother's room—she always kept it locked. After completing his full investigation of the house, he laughed. He called me slick and told me to meet him in the living room. Still standing on top of the stairs, I said no. I ran to the bathroom; I was willing to risk it all. I was going to jump out of the window and into our backyard hopefully landing safely. He began to come back upstairs. Changing my mind about the window, I started to yell. That was a long way down. *Fine. OK. Here I come. Just stop.* Walking in slow motion halfway down the steps, he pulled my arm, rushing me to get down. With a nasty grin and tone in his voice, he said, "Finally you are ten years old, and we are alone."

Trying to fight him for about fifteen minutes, I lost. I was out of breath and tired. Maybe that's why I fought in every relationship I had as an adult. I never really wanted a man to touch me. Slow down, that is not to say I desired a woman to touch me neither. It's no surprise I've been cheated on in every relationship. I could never give a man all of me, especially when I knew he was no good, already cheating, or somebody I didn't see myself with in the long run.

As I got tired of fighting with him, my pants slowly came down. I spit in his face as he did it. I didn't care. I had nothing to lose at this point. The worse thing that could happen to me was happening. Here I was, damaged by what was supposed to be fulfilling to a man and a woman when becoming husband and wife. Was it too much for me to keep my innocence? Was I asking for too much when, as a child, all I wanted was for one man, my husband, to undress me and let my shiver from his touch put to silence all disappointments? Was it too much to just want to save myself for that man, who could leave my satisfaction on the bed sheets? Was I asking for too much? I don't think I was.

After he finished and released himself on top of me, I never felt the same again. I had actually had enough. This was coming to an end. This was going to stop for me. This was not going to be my life. The question became, *what do I do?* He fixed himself and gave me a grand smirk. Hate filled my heart. As he looked at me on his way out, he said, "Next time, I'll leave it in you, and we'll see what happens nine months from now."

He left. I was empty. That was it. My innocence was all I had left, and now that was gone. While he got to live his life in peace, I was left to pick up my pieces. Not knowing how to attach myself back together, I began to place my pieces in the wrong places. My heart was placed under my foot. Stepping on everyone who tried to love me. My head was placed on my shoulders, because I expressed all of my thoughts with my actions. My mouth became a machine. You would have to beat me to quiet me.

My hands became a weapon. Fighting seemed like the solution to everything. The best fights were the ones I didn't start but participated in. I was losing my mind. I remember trying to burn the clothes I had on that day. Too scared to start a fire, I found some scissors, and I cut my clothes into a hundred little pieces. I put them in a bag and walked across the street to the projects and used their dumpster to discard it. Tossing the bag in, I felt my heart leaving me.

~Damaged

Did he just say that to a ten-year-old? Did he just say, "Next time I'll leave it in, and we'll see what happens nine months later," as if I'm fit to be a mother? It was at that moment that I swore to myself I'd never have a man's child. I would never carry a man's seed. That was about the only thing I had left to keep for myself: the child I vowed never to birth. The silence of my child would remind me that I'd succeeded in keeping my one promise to myself: no children, never, in life. I thought to myself that this experience had ruined it for any man that would follow after him. At ten years old, I didn't feel sorry for the thoughts I was having about men. With all I had experienced, I always told myself that a man would never get all of me. I even told myself that I would never get married and live my life with a man for the rest of my life. Well, we know twenty-four years later that this is not how my story ends.

I am a happily married woman with an amazing husband. What's more, I now have six amazing stepchildren. As a ten-year-old, I didn't see this coming. After my experience with him that day, I remember asking myself, *what now?* Go to church on Sunday and continue singing, "He's got the whole world in His hands, He's got the whole wide world in His hands. He's got the little bitty baby in His hands; He's got the whole wide world in His hands?"

I was just about done with that song. I wondered if He'd forgotten about me. Did I slip from His hands? I'd been covered as a child when I fell down the basement steps, but what about now? Surly at ten years old, I still had to mean something to Him, Him being the God of the universe. The way I was being touched. The way life was forcing itself on me.

Where are you now God? Since you see and watch me all day long, since you formed me in my mother's womb, since you know me so well, tell me. Tell me, how is this going to turn out for me. Those where my thoughts then. I felt animosity growing rampant. *And who is to blame? Do I blame myself for this? No. I won't do it. I refuse. This is not my fault. So, whom do I blame? Or is everything just supposed to work out for my good? You tell me. What good am I getting out of this?*

A week later I found myself having to get dress and go to this mans house with family and friends to celebrate his birthday. That was the last thing I wanted to do. His house was packed and still he found a way to get a hold of my little sister. I overheard him speaking asking her to follow him downstairs to his basement, I quickly rushed over.

"No. No. No." I shouted. "No." Go play outside. Go play outside. So, she left, and went outside to play. Oh, he was livid now.

"Abigail, you really know how to piss me off. Now you come with me instead."

He took me to his basement. He stood there jerking himself off. I had to watch. I was boiling on the inside. I was disgusted.

"Let me see you touch yourself," he said.

I had no problem telling him no. Of course, he disliked that. He told me to get closer so I could touch him. But I swear, if I'd had a knife, I would have cut it off. I was starting to hear my little sister. I couldn't make out what she was saying, but she was getting close. I could hear her loud and clear now. She was calling for me. She was yelling my name. To this day, she is my little angel.

I shouted back, "Right here! I'm right here. Here I come. Just stay upstairs."

I ran. I ran upstairs so fast. She may not remember this, but I hugged her so tight, and I whispered in her ear, "*Thank you. Thank you* for calling my name." She was just a kid. She did not know what was going on.

She said, "Abby, I just wanted to play with you."

I couldn't think of a better time to play with her than now.

EXCERPTS FROM MY PERSONAL JOURNAL

What a hell of a few days I've had. And I mean that. This man is sick. Who is telling him that he could do this to me? Instead of my daddy being gone, he should be the one missing. What do I do with this? Do I begin to learn to like it? After all, it's been a few years, and he doesn't seem to have any intentions on stopping. What the hell, man?

I'm so over life. Even regretting my birth, I would rather not exist. Still having to attend church. Still having to believe in God. Not to mention, God is someone I cannot see. Still having to wear this face of peace and happiness while I'm hurting—it's all overrated. Just risk it all, Abby, and run away. Where would I go? Who would believe me? I actually thought about getting on a train and heading to Trenton, New Jersey. My mother, along with my siblings, often takes the Amtrak there. I have plenty of family members in Jersey. Someone will believe me.

Yeah right. That's wishful thinking. I'll never leave. Not because I don't want to, but because I can't afford to leave my little sister alone. I promised myself when she was just a baby that he would never touch her, and I meant that. I'll take it every time if it's going to keep her safe. I actually thought about telling his son, but that quickly changed when I thought, what if he's the same way? That's a conversation not worth having, if that would be the case. I can imagine all the things I'll hear later in life, when this is all out and in the open. I know I'll hear some bogus responses. Some may sound like this: "Oh Abby, you could have come to me. Abby, why didn't you go to the police? Oh, Abby I'm so sorry. Oh, Abby; oh, Abby; oh, Abby."

Oh, please. Save it, all of it. I'm so over this.

Wow!

Can I just break right here and speak as my thirty-four-year-old self? I want my readers to know I am OK. While a lot of this may be hard to read, know that God has kept me. And yes, He still holds the whole world in His hands. No, He didn't forget about me. He never left me or forsook me. He never lost sight of me. While I wish my past experience on no one, I am using it for my good. Those experiences have made their way into a book. Those experiences will be the help that someone else may need. If you are reading this and are struggling with sexual abuse, tell somebody. Tell someone what is happening to you until it stops.

I speak to my ten-year-old self when I say, "This was not your fault. He was a sick man. He had no right to touch you. He had no right to desire you. Your fight was not in vain. You stand here today to tell your story. And the Word is true over your life: 'Greater is He that is in you, than he that is in the world.' Abigail, you are what your name means: beautiful and intelligent."

CHAPTER 6
TELLING MOM

YOU ALL REMEMBER that bike I wanted when I was five years old? Guess what; today was the day. No, I wasn't five, but it's never too late. Mom and I were going to the mall. She said I could pick out any bike I wanted. Getting ready to go, she told my two sisters to get ready as well. Awesome! Family trip. OK, I was overly excited, but, come on, I was finally getting a bike. You have to understand my excitement, especially with how my life was already going. It didn't take much to please me.

We were all ready to go. Elisa, Rebecca, and I were now heading to the door. Going outside, I noticed a very familiar vehicle. My excitement now slowly fading away, I looked at my mother. She handed me some cash for the bike and said, "You girls have fun." *Oh heck no. Wait a minute. What?* Breathless, I stood.

"Mom, you're not coming? Why?"

"You three go and have fun."

Mom mentioned she'd been called in to work, so she called him "the guy" to take us to Franklin Mills Mall instead. In my mind, I was thinking, *Is this her only friend? Is this the only person she knows? She calls him for everything.* While I held my little sister's hand tightly, we got in the car. Elisa sat in the front, while Rebecca and I sat in the back. For once I did not have to sit next to him, but I did not want my sister to have to sit up front with him neither. I watched his every move without alerting my siblings. When he went to turn up the radio, I flinched and balled up my fist. When he went to turn the air on, I flinched. Each time he made a sudden moved, I flinched. I was ready if he tried to touch my sister's knee. But he didn't. At the mall, I was no longer excited. I was too tense. We spent about two hours at the mall. He purchased whatever Rebecca wanted or pointed to; I guess he was fulfilling his godfather duties. I did purchase a bike, finally. Sitting in the food court was awkward. I remember sitting at a round table making small talk. As I watched him study me, smiling from ear to ear, I found myself losing my appetite. I wanted to vomit. That was how disgusted I was with him. The thought of him made me sick; his presence was worse. Everyone was done eating, and I was hoping we would leave. Swallowing his last bite of the burger, he said those magic words: "Let's go." This was the best part of the trip; him taking us home.

Heading back to the car, Elisa walked before me, with him by her side. I trailed behind her with my bike, but now my mind was beginning to play tricks on me. Had I seen that right? Did he just try to touch my sister's breast? Walking through the parking lot to the car, he did it again. What I was seeing was real. He touched my sister on her breast again. Watching her slap his hand away pissed me off. If I could throw this bike at him and get away with it, I would. I was furious. It was a silent drive home. I was determined to tell my mother, yet again, what was happening to us with this man. We arrived at the house. I quickly got out of the car, removed my bike from the trunk, and wasting no time, I flew in the house. My other two sisters followed. He never did come inside. Noticing my mother in the dining room, I quickly told her that I needed to speak with her. She didn't look like she wanted to be bothered, but I just started spilling the beans.

"It's him. He touches us, and I do not want him around us anymore. He's been touching me for a while. And I do not want him near me. I don't need any rides from him, food from him—nothing."

I stood there, out of breath, waiting for my mother to respond, but she just accused me of lying. *Again.*

I can't tell you how that made me feel. Lying?

I shouted back, "Mom, what is there to lie about? After all I have gone through with him. Why would you think I would be lying?"

Still, she insisted I was lying. Let me just pause right here and get this out of the bag, since I haven't brought it up. *So, you're home,* I'm thinking to myself. *Why are you even home, because what sense did that make for you not to come with us to the mall? If your job called you in, why are you still home?* But since I had never asked the question, I didn't have an answer. And at this point, I didn't think I would ever ask.

As my mother just accused me of lying my sister spoke up. She was a witness. More like a victim. "She's not lying, Mom." Elisa stated.

Now, I don't think she knew anything that had been going on with me, but since she had been touched too, in a way, she could protest that I was not lying. My mother, now looking concerned, told us to go upstairs. So we went. But we didn't go too far. She reached for the house phone in the dining room, and we listened from the steps. Immediately, she called him. We could hear the conversation from the top of the steps.

"You touched my daughters? They both are telling me that you have touched them. I trusted you with my daughters. You were just supposed to watch over them. You were never supposed to touch any of them. Don't come on Monday. Don't pick her up for school."

Even with only one half of the conversation we could tell he denied it all. Wow. I couldn't believe he had really just denied touching us. But then again, why would he confirm that he was? After that conversation, my mother didn't say much for the rest of the day. But I was ready to tell it all. I could tell she couldn't take any more than what we'd already told her. There wasn't much conversation about it with my sister. We kind of just let it go.

I felt like a load had been lifted off of me that day. It was good to know that, at least, I wouldn't have to see him this weekend and he wouldn't be around on Monday. I would take this weekend to relax, knowing I didn't have to see him for a while. To help get my mind off things, I wiped my bike down and went for a ride. Surprisingly I did well. I say surprisingly because I'd never ridden a bike before. I only had two, three, or ten falls here and there, but besides that, I believe I did well. Riding got easier over the next two weeks. There were fewer falls, but I was up to forty-eight scratches on my brand-new helmet in just two weeks.

One random Wednesday, I remember riding my bike outside. I had one hour to ride before having to get ready for Bible study. My brother was outside with me. I asked him to watch the bike while I went into the house to use the restroom. Rushing up the steps, not wanting to leave my bike out of sight, I quickly did what was needed; I washed my hands, and back outside I went. I didn't see my brother or the bike. I figured he'd taken it for a ride. He was kind of big for it, but hey, what other explanation was there? I sat on the steps for about ten minutes before I noticed my brother coming out of the projects. But there was no bike with him. He got closer and closer and closer, then I asked, "Bro where is my bike?"

With no expression on his face, he just shrugged his shoulders as if to indicate he didn't know where my bike was.

Now wait, that wasn't OK. I said again, "Bro my bike. Where is it?"

And just like that, he stated that it must have gotten stolen while he went into the projects.

I was just trying to understand why he was in the projects after our mother had told him numerous times to stop going over there—because their elevators didn't work too well, and every day someone was getting stuck. His friends lived on the fifteenth floor, so he was always getting on the elevators. So, since he allowed my bike to get stolen let me do this…

MESSAGE TO MOM

Junie used to always go across the street to the projects; when you went to work, when you went to nursing school, he was always over there. What's more, he almost got stuck on those same elevators you told him not to use. But somehow, he always managed to get back across the street before you got home.

There. I said it. I told. And I still don't have a bike, so snitching was pointless. We are all grown now; I'm sure we'll just laugh this part out.

But seriously, now I had to explain to my mother that the new bike was gone. Stolen. Taken. Out of sight. Not feeling confident about this conversation at all, I went to my mother's room and explained to her that my bike had already gotten stolen. She asked what had happened; I didn't bother mentioning my brother. I just told her that I'd needed to use the restroom and I'd left my bike outside unattended. She looked at me with the look of death. If looks could kill, I would be dead. I was waiting for her to say something. I guess she didn't feel like being disturbed today; she only said, "That's your fault. I'm not buying you another one." Not really expecting her to buy me another bike, I said OK and that I was sorry. That was it. It took forever for me to get a bike, and it took no time for it to get stolen.

EXCERPTS FROM MY PERSONAL JOURNAL

Today could have been the day I expressed to my mother my unspoken truth. But to spare her feelings, I didn't. How much longer would I have to do that? Spare someone else's feelings while burying my pain. It's impossible to keep burying something that is alive. It will only keep resurrecting. There's no letting this go. I'm tired. But I'm not letting up, because I'm too young to keep all of this in. This is the type of stuff that kids hurt themselves over. Suicide is real. And I don't want to be one of those kids that end up hanging themselves and cutting their wrist. I have a few friends that normally cut themselves at least once a week. I'm not sure whether they're trying to die or get attention, but either way, I just don't see myself hurting, cutting, or hanging myself due to lack of attention. All I'm saying is that I understand why some kids and teenagers do it. I'm not trying to be one of those kids. God has given me crazy strength, strength to deal with a lot and strength to fight a lot. I just want to know at what point this all stops. I'm glad I have these next few days off from seeing "the guy." I don't even have the guts to mention his name. As if I'm trying to protect him. Saying his name will just make it too real, although it can't get any more real than this.

CHAPTER 7
THE RELIEF

THESE WORDS THAT my mother spoke were music to my ears: "I am taking you to see your father today."

Oh, how I'd longed to hear those words. After everything that had happened to me, I was ready to see and speak with my father. I was moving at about 100 miles per hour now. I was rushing to shower and get dressed. Best day of my life. I was excited. I was overjoyed. I was happy. Then I had a question: "Mom, you know where he's at? This whole time, you knew where he's been?"

I don't even know why I thought I would get an answer. She simply said, "We leaving in an hour. Be ready or get left."

Thinking back over this specific day, I have to laugh. And people wondered where I got my attitude and sarcasm. As the good old saying goes, "the apple doesn't fall far from the tree." But I'll move on from this. Today was the day I would tell my daddy everything. A few of my siblings got in the car with my mom and me. We drove for about an hour or two before my mother stated we had arrived. I was not shocked. I was just disappointed, I guess. This was what I did not want to believe. Entering into the facility, all you heard was, "Remove all metal, belts, and electronics from your pockets before coming through." I walked right through the metal detectors. We were all in the waiting area when suddenly a loud buzz peeled out. I covered my ears, as they were running a sixty-second test. That was the longest sixty seconds of my life. The gate was opening. *Papi! Papi! Papi!* I was going through the second metal detector, rushing to get to my father, when suddenly we were held up.

"Wait here. You might not be able to come in."

What? The officer was not talking to me, but he was talking to my sister Elisa. She'd decided to wear black tights today. How were we supposed to know there was a dress code? We had no idea. We barely even knew where we were going. Ugh. So now we waited another ten minutes because of miss little black tights over there. Ten minutes went by, and they finally allowed us to go through. I ran to my daddy, and I hugged him so tightly. I did not want to let go. He spoke with my siblings and me for a little while. I was just waiting for my one-on-one time, but then my mother mentioned she needed to speak with him alone. I could not imagine what for. They spoke for about fifteen minutes. Their conversation was over, and ours was just beginning. I was ready to tell my daddy everything when suddenly an officer yelled, "Five minutes left. Five minutes left. Wrap it up. Visitors have five minutes left." I was thinking, *Shut up with your yelling. You guys are wasting my last five minutes.* Of course, I did not say that out loud. I was just thinking it.

Well, certainly five minutes was not enough. My heart sank. I knew I wouldn't get to tell him on this trip. Still sitting up with my back straight, I asked when I would be able to see him again. He stated it was up to my mother, since she would have to bring me. I looked at my mother and asked when we would be returning, and of course, she gave me nothing but attitude.

"I don't know," she said. Well that was that. I didn't know when would be the next time, I'd get to see him. Didn't anyone know that all I was trying to do was tell my story and get this pain out of my chest? Like, why was telling this horrible experience to my parents so difficult? Now I was leaving the prison with mixed emotions. It was great to see him, but I wish I'd had more time.

The ride back home was long and quiet for me. I had nothing to say. I took all of my feelings, and I pushed them back down again. Not letting anyone notice something was wrong with me, I just closed my eyes and pretended I was sleep. If I could have burst into tears, I would have. But I'd been strong up to this point; I wouldn't let up now. I figured I'd just try to come up with something else to think about but that was not working. Replays of my experience were beginning to play in my head. My private screams with that man were now my daily mental thoughts. As we drove down the road, I felt my skin roasting. I was becoming angry all over again. If I didn't get this stuff off of me, I was going to explode. Could this be the way of life? People often say that pain to this degree comes just to make one stronger. While I was strong physically, it was beginning to weaken my mind. This was all I was thinking about, every single day. This couldn't be good for me.

It was the last week of middle school. I couldn't believe it. I was on my way to Dobbins Randolph High School. At least, that was the school I was hoping to get accepted to. I was so excited. Graduation was in just a few days! While leaving Elverson Middle School and making my way home, I noticed a car driving slowly beside me. It was an unfamiliar car. So I stopped. I did not panic. I had no fear. At this point in my life, not only did personal circumstances make me tough, but also the streets of North Philly put no fear in me. I turned around to see who it was. I wasn't even surprised. It had been a while. It was "the guy."

"Get in; I have a surprise for you."

I laughed. I thought to myself, I've seen it all. You come with no great surprises. Your package is small. All of me wanted to burst out laughing from my internal conversation, but I smirked instead. I quickly straightened up as I saw a shadow in the back seat of his minivan. Wait, this shadow, this image, looked like my father. I hopped into his minivan, turned to the back seat, and there he was. My daddy. I just fell into his arms. It was my father. We drove to my mother's house. After we parked, my father said to the man, "I need time with my daughter."

So, he left us to be alone. I yelled, "Daddy, you're home! I'm so happy to see you."

But before I could say another word, my father looked at me and said, "I know."

I sat there frozen. I did not know what to say or if I should say anything at all. So I waited. Waited some more. Then finally my daddy spoke.

He said in a low, sweet voice, "I know you've been touched, but I promise you, I'm home now. No one, and I mean no one, will ever touch you like that again. I am fully aware of what he's done to you, daughter. But I'll handle it from here. After today, you'll never have to see him again."

I rested my head on my daddy's shoulder and cried. All I could say was, "Welcome home, Daddy. Welcome home!" I wiped the tears from my eyes and headed into the house. "Mom, Mom! There's a surprise here for you."

"Surprise? What is it?"

It did not take long for her to notice my father. "Get out!" she shouted. "Get out! Who let you out of prison? This is not a good surprise. Get out!"

Why was my mother always so angry with my father? I just could not put my finger on it. Why wouldn't she let up? There had to be more to this. But whatever it was, I was unaware of it.

My father didn't make himself at home; rather, we sat outside, trying to catch up. We talked about everything: school, sports, and church. I noticed "the guy" was really uncomfortable. This day was different. He didn't try to touch me, not one time. He didn't sit next to me; as a matter of fact, after getting out of his minivan, he didn't say another word to me. Now, that was odd.

My conversation with my father was great. He caught me up on what had happened on the day we went to go get milk, bread, and eggs. The guys at the corner of thirteenth and York did hold him up. They checked out his dice and saw they were "dirty" (a street word for bad), but for some reason, they let him go. It was after they let him go that he went on and got into some more trouble with some other guys for playing with those same hand carved dice. Those guys didn't take it too well. Cops were called, and a few were locked up, my father in the number. The story got more interesting when Dad mentioned Neal's name. He stated that Neal had been one of the guys playing dice with him when the cops were called. Neal was one of guys who outran the cops. And here I was, trying to get help from Neal when he knew all along exactly what happened to my father. Wow.

After an hour, my mother called me into the house. Dinner was ready, and she wanted to know if my father wanted a plate. She said he could eat, but he couldn't come inside. This family of mine was getting crazier by the minute. Of course, my father was hungry. She made him a big plate. She asked if "the guy" was hungry, and without even asking him, I told my mother he was not hungry. So, while my father and I ate on the steps, "the guy" sat in the car.

Writing this out makes it seem so mean, but at the time, I was totally fine with it. Wrapping it up with my father, I asked where he would go for the night, since my mother had made it clear that he was not allowed back in the house. He said he would stay at the halfway house on Lehigh Ave. I wasn't too fond of the place, but at least he wouldn't be far.

Before my father left, I gave him a look. It was a strong look. I needed him to know that I needed to speak with him alone without "the guy" around. But I didn't have to say anything.

All he said was, "I know, daughter. I know."

It was at that moment that I was convinced my father knew everything and I could stand on the truth of never seeing "the guy" again.

EXCERPTS FROM MY PERSONAL JOURNAL

I don't know how. I don't know when. But my daddy knows everything. He knew "the guy" had touched me. I'm starting to think maybe that was the conversation my mother had with him for fifteen minutes at the prison when we went to see him not too long ago. But I'm not certain. I honestly cannot think of another way he could have known. Spending time with my father today was priceless. There's nothing better I could be asking for, even as a graduation gift. Something about having my daddy around made me feel protected. I just hope my daddy is here to stay. Knowing that I won't ever have to see "the guy" again brings peace over me. But how do I begin to heal? If both my parents know what has happened to me, then what is the process to help me?

This is the problem with parents. They know, but they don't do anything about it. Knowing is not enough. We need help. We children are screaming for help. But if the parents are not willing to face our truth and reality, then how do they expect us to heal and move pass this? Am I just supposed to brush this off? We'll I can't. I've been damaged since I was seven years old. I'm fourteen years old now and heading into high school. When does my healing begin so I can begin to live my life? I've been living my life trying to protect others and be there for others, but whom can I talk to about my entire experience? It doesn't seem like I can go to anyone. And at this point, I think I'll be embarrassing my parents if I try to bring it up to another adult.

Lord, I know I can talk to you. And I have been talking to you. I just want to know what I have to do to begin healing. Speaking about this and healing from this are two different things. I want to speak on it, but more than anything, I want to heal from this. But how?

CHAPTER 8
THE POISON

DAD CAME TO visit with jewelry and gifts. He was allowed in the house, just not upstairs. My mother didn't want him snooping around. If he wanted to hang around or even rest his head for a little while, he had to do it in the basement. The basement had pretty much become his home. I was just happy to see him more often. The gifts were a nice surprise. The watches, rings, and necklaces were all so beautiful. He also gave me four different-colored watchbands. I could change the band out every day to match my outfits if I wanted to. I didn't ask any questions about where any of this had come from. I knew he wasn't working and hadn't hit the lottery, so that only left one other explanation. My mind was curious though. I couldn't stop thinking about where it might've come from. *Lord have mercy. I can only imagine.* Knowing better not to ask, I said thank you and went on my way.

Five hours went by, and there was a knock on the door. I answered. There stood a woman. I'd never seen her before. Looking so pale as if she had just seen a ghost, she just stared at me. Rather, my wrist transfixed her.

"My watch!" She announced. And she actually stuck her hand out as if I was just going to allow her to take it off my wrist. Was she crazy?

"Excuse me. How can I help you?"

She went on to say, "Little girl, the watch you are wearing belongs to me. Do you have the colorful bands that go with it?"

Angry, I shouted back, "Did you just come to my doorstep calling me a little girl? Woman, you don't know me, and I don't know what you are talking about, but this right here is my watch."

My mother came to the door.

"Can I help you?" My mother said.

"Yes, actually you can. If this is your daughter, she is wearing my watch. It was stolen from me. A few days ago, a man entered my house. I was poisoned. After my recovery, I thought to view the cameras that I have around my house. I haven't gone to the police yet, but a friend of mine said that the man in the camera, the man that did this to me, lives here. He stole from me. He tried to kill me. And your daughter has on my watch. I want it back. Is he your husband?"

My mother did not seem surprised by any of this and definitely ignored all of the questions. While they exchanged conversation, I peeked my head outside and realized this woman had not come alone. There were two guys leaning on a car right outside of the house. They had to been 6'2 weighing 240-250lbs. So, I ran into the basement, where my father was, and told him to run because some woman was here to hurt him and she wasn't alone. I didn't even have to explain why she was here. The way my father got up indicated he had done exactly what she was saying he'd done. My father ran up the basement steps and out the kitchen door, which lead to the backyard. I ran behind him to sit on top of the stairs with my sister Elisa.

Suddenly, we heard, "There he is."

The women at the door had seen my father leaving the basement and running toward the kitchen. She yelled, "He's here! He's here!"

The two big guys ran through our house, almost knocking my mother over. They ran through our kitchen door just to be trapped in our backyard. They weren't aware that we had a padlock in our gate. The only way to get over was to jump the high fence like my daddy had done. Did they really think he was going to leave the gate unlocked for them? I laughed as I heard one of the guys say, "Lift me up; lift me up."

Eventually, they got over the fence. Unfortunately for them, they never caught my daddy. I guess they had to be quicker than that. The woman was still standing at the door, waiting to receive her watch, and she looked at me as I stayed at the top of the steps. My mother called me back down, and of course, she made me take it off and return the colorful bands as well. I gave the lady back her watch, but I was not happy about it. She, on the other hand was ecstatic to have it back in her possession.

"Whatever, lady," I whispered underneath my breath. I seriously had an attitude problem at this point. But can you blame me? I'd had one heck of a ride, all before the age of fifteen. I didn't give the lady the rings and necklaces that my daddy had given me. I just gave her what she asked for: the watch and the colorful bands. Since she never mentioned the rings and necklaces, I began to wonder if they might have come from two different households. That was a possibility. Anything was possible with my father. The two guys were now at our front door. Out of breath, they told her they couldn't find him. I just shook my head. *How do you come to an unfamiliar environment and expect to keep up? You'll never catch or find my father. Go back to Fifth and Allegheny were you probably came from*—these thoughts kept running through my head. After the woman left, my mother was hot. That was the last straw; my father would no longer have any access to the house. He really wasn't allowed back inside.

Side note: Sometimes people destroy their front door access when they can't give up their bad habits. ~Abigail Couzens

A few weeks went by, and there was still no sign of my father. I felt like I'd fallen into some type of depression. Not because I had a mental problem (because I didn't) but simply because of life stressors. I'd been stressed for a few years now, and I'd learned how to hide it so well. I could almost guarantee that, if I ever told my story, people would truly say, "You don't look like what you've been through." For that, I am grateful.

Sitting outside catching a breeze, I noticed my father coming down the street. Getting straight to the point, I asked, "Who were those guys a few weeks ago at Mom's house? What did you do to that lady? Is it true what she said? Did you try to kill her?"

On and on I went with the questions. My father did not answer a single question; instead, he just stood there, hands on the stroller.

"Wait. Let me ask a better question. Who is that in the stroller? Why are you pushing a stroller?"

His response just about blew my mind.

"Here's a sister, but not from your mother."

"Who? What? When? Where? How? Did I mention *what*?"

He went on to say that this was one of the reasons why "*I guess* your mother hates me so much."

"*You guess*," I shouted back.

He went on to say that he wasn't faithful and he'd thought his time in prison away from my mother would make him realize just how much he loved and needed her. But nope, another sister from another woman. I couldn't wait to tell my other siblings this. I still had questions, so I asked, "Who is the mother? Do we know her? Does Mom know her?"

My father said we did not know who she was and that was all he would say about it. *Well, all right. Good to know our family has great communication skills. There you have it, another sister from another woman.*

Some of you may be saying, "Wow, that's baby number seven." But it is not. It's actually baby number nine. Yes. Nine. My father already had two children before marrying my mother. I was thinking, *just have one more so we can be a team of ten, why don't you.*

(It has actually been said that there were ten of us. But no one has ever confirmed it, so I'll stick to nine. There were now nine of us.)

My mother now yelling for me from across the street, so I ran back to see what she needed from me. Was that her? Was that his daughter? Yes. Yes, that was his daughter. It was my first time seeing her or even hearing about her mom.

Oh my gosh, talk about pressure. I didn't know what would happen next. Mom continued, "Tell him to get out of this block with that stroller."

If I could have ripped my head off, I think I would have at this moment. When was life going to show me balance? What I had experienced up to this point was only disappointment and mess. This couldn't be life for me. And I would keep saying that until life changed for me. I ran back across the street to my daddy.

"You have to leave. Mom doesn't want to see you on this block with this baby. You have to go. Take her home, wherever that is, and then come back."

Daddy just said he'd see everyone later.

"OK," I said. Down the street he went with the stroller. I told my older siblings the news, and they were not shocked or surprised. It was more of a "I don't care" type of attitude. Had they already known? I hadn't.

EXCERPTS FROM MY PERSONAL JOURNAL

Another baby. Another baby. This father of mine is a rolling stone indeed. I guess when my momma kicked him out, he found a place to rest his head. My goodness. I want to know who the mother is to this child. Not because I want or need a conversation, but I just want to know. And what was my father thinking when he decided to rob that woman? Normally people rob other people to sell what they are able to collect. Not my daddy. He wanted to give it to us as gifts. It would have been easier to hide money than to hide a watch that is worn. I'm not saying what he did was right. I'm just saying, you don't rob somebody then keep the treasure. You pawn it or something.

My experience with the woman at the door was beginning to show me how my past experiences were forming my attitude and my engagement with strangers. I was beginning to realize that I had zero tolerance for people I did not know. I was shocked because, outside of this woman, I was a kind and loving person to others. I am beginning to notice that a guard goes up immediately when I feel I am being attacked. I know where it comes from. This comes from telling myself that I will never be taken advantage of again, in any way whatsoever. Could this be a safe development for me? Whether it's safe or not, I trust who I trust, and I love who I love. I'm learning to keep my circle tight. Only a handful of people will actually be willing to protect you. While others may say they love you and will be there for you, I've learned, just being fifteen years old, that actions speak louder than words. And let me tell you, I've come across some people who showed their true colors. And when someone shows you their true colors the first time, believe them. But right about now, I wouldn't care if they were coming or going. My thought process at fifteen years old was this: if I've gone fifteen years without you, bet your last dollar I'll do another fifteen without you and not think twice about it. That was my mindset at just fifteen years old. And speaking as my thirty-four-year-old self, I can honestly say, its not difficult letting people go. I've seen people leave and begin to act differently because my situation was too difficult for them. I've experienced the shift. I've been there and done that. I've learned as a fifteen-year-old coming out of my toughest years in life what a true ride-a-die is. It's being there even when you don't agree. Its being there at one's lowest and speaking life back into them.

It was during my teenage years that my courage, fight for life, and loyalty to people were being developed. Even now, you could ask anyone from my inner Philly circle (because the squad is the same) to describe me in one word, and his or her word would be *loyal.* I know what it means to be there for someone, even if it's uncomfortable. "How? you may be asking." Because from ages seven to fifteen, that was all I needed. I needed someone to be there, to help me, to protect me, even while it was uncomfortable. It's no surprise I'm overprotective of my husband, stepchildren, parents, siblings, and my Philly squad. It's no surprise. It's been built into me. I am that ride-a-die!

CHAPTER 9
LOSING DADDY AGAIN

"I WILL BE right back," my father said as Rebecca and I played outside.

"Where you going?"

I was always asking questions. Sometimes I got no answer, but it was always better to ask.

"To the corner store to buy you all some chips and snacks," is what he said.

"Great. Get me some Red Hot Chips, some grape Now and Laters, and a Slim Jim."

To this day, these are still my favorites. About an hour went by, and still no chips, Now and Laters, or Slim Jims. Instead, a cop car pulled up to the house. Who was sitting in the backseat? My dad. But why? Why was he in cuffs? *Here we go.*

The officer stepped out of the vehicle and mentioned she was bringing him around so he could say goodbye. She went on to say how my father had pleaded with her to come to the house because he had two daughters waiting on him. I guess that touched her heart, so she made a stop to the house. I asked what had happened. My father shouted from the back seat not to worry, that he was OK, and that someone tried to rob him in the corner store.

Come on now. Even I knew better than that. That made no sense to me whatsoever. I went with it. I said, "So if someone tried to rob you (emphasizing you) at the corner store, why are you in handcuffs?"

I guess he didn't see that question coming. He just laughed and said it would be OK and that he would be back. Well, there went my daddy again. I thanked the officer and went back to the steps. At least, this time I didn't have to sit by the window waiting for him to come around. I knew where he was going. I just rolled my shoulders back, wiped my tears, and keep pushing. I was hoping to have my Daddy around before I started High School, which was starting in just a few days. I guess not.

Rebecca was not holding up too well. She really wanted her candy. Poor thing. I was used to this kind of thing. Up till this age of fifteen, I had seen and heard it all. I'd learned to adjust my attitude to whatever life threw at me on a day-to-day basis. With my attitude getting worse, my sister Carmen thought it would be best for me to join her in church. I was not for it. She told me that, one day, God would use that same attitude that I had for the streets and would use it for the Kingdom.

Again, I was not trying to hear any of it. But then it happened; after months of her inviting me to church, I finally said yes. I don't know about you, but although I stand here today saved, sanctified, and filled with the precious Holy Ghost, something about wearing dresses to my knees and ankles twenty-four, seven is not OK with me. Sunday after Sunday, I just kept hearing what *not* to do. *Don't wear earrings. Don't wear pants. Don't wear makeup. Don't walk up in here thinking you too cute. Don't do this. Don't do that.* I was over it. Although I have created a lifelong relationship with some of the members there, I never want to have that type of "church experience" ever again.

I eventually became a member of the church and joined a few ministries. I joined the choir and the performance arts ministry, and when I really got into it, I began to teach Sunday school. My sister was right. That same attitude and energy I had for the streets shifted to praise and worship. I praise dance for ten years. I had one of the best partners I could ever ask for. We performed in other churches and often put on plays. Us performing together was powerful. She is one that I still talk to every single day. Literally. Every single day, we communicate with each other. And I guess we have to, since we are doing a 365-day devotional together. So, we have no other choice. My Dog!

Getting ready to start a new journey in life; High school! Clothes are ironed, hair in tact, missing one person; my Daddy. A day doesn't go by that I am caught thinking of him. Man, I miss him. Right now I must go on. This is my time to become creative, an innovator. Dobbins Randolph Tech. Located at Twenty-Second and Lehigh. This was my number-one high school pick. I was so excited I'd gotten in. What's more, my middle school principal was now my high school principal; it worked for me. We got along well in middle school. I was a White William Scholar, made the National Honor Society, and spoke at meetings with the major of Philadelphia in attendance. I did well in middle school. I wanted to see what this new school year would bring. Oh, but I didn't think about the boys; they were coming on a little strong over here. There's definitely a difference between how an eighth grader approaches you and how a senior in high school approaches you.

"Hey light bright. Hey snowflake. Hey smalls. Hey petite." Like what? Were they serious? This was just day one, and I'd already been given about ten nicknames. As long as none of them touched me, I was perfectly fine.

Heading into my shop class (which I would have for the next four years), it seemed like fun. Baking. Dobbins Randolph was a tech school. It was one name with two locations. Dobbins was its own building, and Randolph was its own building. But each building had shop classes. We at Dobbins had fashion design, cosmetology, culinary arts, baking, and so much more. I must say, those were the best four years of my life. We baked everything from danishes to macaroons; you name it, we baked it. All from scratch. The students in my shop were cool. One in particular became my best friend.

"Hello," said someone from behind me.

I turned around. "Hi, we in here for the next four years."

We both laughed.

"I'm Moe."

"Hey, Moe. I'm Abby."

And so our friendship took off. That was back in 2000. Twenty years later, and we are still close. As mentioned, more like best friends. We've laughed together, traveled together, and even cried together (we'll get to that part a little later). I participated in almost every activity I could think of. Basketball, volleyball, cheerleading, and most importantly, softball. Between our men's baseball and our women's softball team, we were the best. Senior year, I made the National Honor Society. I was also a White William Scholar and senior class president. High school was one of the best times of my life. Prom was approaching, and I was excited about it. I was taking my sister Elisa with me. This would be a great time.

It was prom 2004. I was standing outside taking pictures with all of my friends, family members, and neighbors when suddenly my mother began to embarrass me, yelling and pointing the finger. *Great.* Just what I needed. I ran into the house. My sisters ran behind me.

"Don't let Mom ruin your special evening, Abby," my older sister Sandra said. "Don't let Mom ruin this for you. You worked so hard all year long. This is your year. Wipe your eyes and go back outside. Say bye to your friends. Your driver is here; just get in the vehicle and go."

So, I did just that. I wiped my face and got my sister Elisa, and we went back outside and got in the vehicle. This had not just happened to me, right? I hadn't just been embarrassed in front of all of my friend's, right? Yes. I had been. But I had my entire prom night ahead of me. I wouldn't let this stop me.

Finally, we arrived at prom. Everyone was looking beautiful. The glam dresses, the suits and ties—it was perfect. About thirty minutes into the prom, I was searching for my sister. She was nowhere to be found. I mean nowhere. "Have you seen my sister? Have you seen Elisa?" Those were my questions to a few classmates. I looked for her for the next forty-five minutes. Suddenly, she appeared out of nowhere, just smiling as if nothing was wrong. As if she just wasn't MIA for forty-five minutes. Here I was, worried and in tears.

"Elisa, where were you?"

"I was on the phone."

"You were on the phone? That's it? Elisa, I've been looking everywhere for you for the past forty-five minutes, and all you have to say is you were on the phone?"

"Sis, let's not talk about this right now. It's your prom night. Enjoy it."

"I'm so confused. Nothing about this night is enjoyable; please just tell me what is going on. Elisa, is everything alright?"

I pressed the issue until she spilled it.

"It's Mom. Abby she's not happy and she is trying to get a hold of you."

"Mom? Why would she be trying to get a hold of me? What have I done now?"

"Abby, Mom is yelling and just losing it. She wants to talk to you, but I won't let her because it's your special night, so just enjoy yourself with your friends."

This was truly one night to remember. With no one realizing that my life was in a million pieces, I continued to hold my head up and took picture after picture. I don't even know how I was able to manage a smile throughout the night. My heart was so heavy. I asked my sister if I could use her phone to make one call. Who did I call? My daddy. He was in Puerto Rico at the time. He was scheduled to arrive in Philly in a few days for my graduation. When I was done pouring myself out to him, he assured me I would see him before graduation day. He wasn't sure how, but he said he would be in Philly sooner than expected. That helped with my night until I got home. All hell broke loose. I just couldn't catch a break. How much more was I supposed to take before it took me out? There in my room was a note from my mother: "Get Out!"

I couldn't believe this. Where was I supposed to go? I'd just turned eighteen and was just a few days from graduation. Where was I supposed to go? She had already packed a few of my things. There were trash bags all over my room. I didn't waste any more time. I was tired. I was tired of fighting. I was tired of wanting to be loved. I filled up the trash bags with as much stuff as I could. I could hear her getting up. I could hear her footsteps. I quickly grabbed a bag and ran downstairs.

"Abigail, get out!" she was shouting, and I was tired of crying, so I flew out the door. But where was I going? What had I done to truly deserve any of this? I mean, really. My sister Elisa had a car. Good thing I actually knew how to drive and had my license. Elisa ran out the house behind me. She called for me and as I began to turn around all I seen were some keys flying in the air. She threw me her car keys. I swear, it felt like a scene out of a movie. I caught the keys in midair and ran toward her car. My mother was now yelling; I could barely understand her.

All I understood was "Get out."

All I understood was *hate*.

All I understood was that I wasn't wanted, and I wasn't wanted by her, my mother. I wouldn't wish my pain that night upon any child.

Rushing to start my sister's car, I took off quickly. *Where do I go?* I made one stop. I banged so hard on her door.

"Who is it? Who is banging on my door at three o'clock in the morning?"

Those were the words of my best friend, Moe. I was standing there with tears in my eyes. Still wearing my prom dress. I fell into her arms.

"Moe, why does she hate me? Why did she do this to me tonight? She could have waited till after graduation. Where am I supposed to go?"

Moe tried so hard to get me under control.

"Abby, you can stay here. Let's come inside."

I was such a mess, I never made it into the house. We sat in the car, and I just cried until I had nothing left in me. My sister Elisa called, and she wanted to know where I was.

I told her I wasn't too far. I was at Moe's house. She told me that our older sister Carmen was expecting me. So, I wiped my face and told Moe I had to go. Not letting me go that easy, Moe said, "Hold up. We both going."

You can probably see why she's my best friend. From there, we both headed to my sister's house at 3:00 a.m. We arrived, and no words were needed. Space was already prepared for us to sleep. We just passed out. Neither one of us had anything to say besides goodnight.

———

The next morning, Moe and I just looked at each other.

I said, "I'm tired of covering up my hurts. I'm tired of pretending I'm all right. Nothing is right. Nothing has been right for years."

Moe looked at me and said, "We still going to Six Flags?"

We both burst out laughing. Six Flags was where everybody went after prom. My situation did not stop the fun. The weekend arrived, and we loaded a car, and to Six Flags Great Adventures we went. It was a great time. We ran into so many of our classmates. Heading back to Philly from Six Flags, guess who I saw? That's right. My daddy. He made it happen. I told him everything. Through my tears, my pain, my hurt. I finally released it all. I'd always wanted to ask him what had happened to that "man," because, just like he'd said, I had never seen him again.

EXCERPTS FROM MY PERSONAL JOURNAL

I couldn't even write for the first fifteen minutes. I just stared at this paper, thinking that it would write itself. How great it would have been for my thoughts and feelings to just appear on this sheet. But they didn't. I had to force myself to pick up this pen. Yes, the pen I am using to write this down. I forced myself to write out all of my feelings. Every time I began to cry, I balled up the paper and started again. This is about my seventh time starting over. I was not going to allow myself to cry this out. I refuse. I haven't caught a break yet, maybe after high school, I'll be on my own, away from everybody and maybe I'll catch a break then. Being thrown out of the house with my prom dress still on was terrible. While my classmates were sleeping after a night of dance and laughter, there I was trying to figure out where I would be resting my head for the night.

It amazes me how strong I am. If I was to die and someone was to find this journal, they wouldn't believe it. Their mouth would be dropped to the floor, but it's all true. Trying now to prepare my speech for graduation, all I've got down so far is "Class of 2004." I've been looking at those few words for the past hour. I don't even have enough strength to come up with anything. How can I encourage them? What could I possibly say? I have nothing.

CHAPTER 10
GRADUATION DAY 2004

I'D NEVER THOUGHT I would have to start my big day with this question; unfortunately, I had to.

"Is Mom coming to my graduation?" I sadly asked my siblings.

They mentioned they weren't sure. That pierced my heart in an unexplainable way. But I knew I had to continue on with my day. As senior class president, I walked onto the stage and took my seat. I held my head up high and smiled at everyone I came in contact with. I was able to pinpoint my family in the stands. There they sat, to the right of me. Perfect view. Now I was asking myself, *Is that who I think it is? Yes, it is. Why am I getting so nervous? Stay calm, Abby, stay calm.* It was my mother. She'd come. I'm trying to hold back my tears as I share this piece of my journey with you, but I can't.

My mother came to my graduation. While it may have been normal for other graduates to have their mothers present, to have mine was a miracle. While many may not consider this a big deal, trust me when I say it was my big deal. I sat up straight. I looked over my speech; I couldn't mess up now that my mother was here. Maybe if I said everything right, she would be proud of me. Here I went; time to say my speech. Before I started my speech, it all hit me. What would life look like for me after I got off of this platform?

Where would I go? College was not an option for me. At least, not right now. Maybe I would go into the Air Force. Maybe, if I followed my brother's footsteps, I would go into the US Navy; maybe then, she would be proud.

While I stood with so many uncertainties, I still held on to the one truth I knew: "He's got the whole world in His hands. He's got the whole wide world in His hands." Those are the words to the song that popped up into my head at that moment. Certainly, there was room in God's hands for me, right? Continuing with my speech, I asked for a moment of silence as we gave honor and respect to our fallen seniors. We cried, then we cheered. I was able to make it through. I wrapped it up, took my seat, and felt proud of my accomplishments. This day proved my strength and determination. I'd done it. Through all my hurt, pain, and unanswered questions, I'd done it. Still uncertain of what would be next, I began to have those conversations with myself.

Since my mother had kicked me out of the house, I knew that going back was not an option. I had nothing at my mother's house, and I hoped this brought her the peace and happiness that she was seeking.

But then again, what was she seeking? Why did she have it out for me? Had I truly been that bad of a kid growing up? I mean, with all I'd been through, I liked to think I'd done the best I could holding it all in. Not telling a soul and still keeping up with my grades, sports, and having a good social life. Friends were never hard to come by. I was funny, outgoing, loving, and loyal. Why was everyone else around me seeing me for who I was and could become, except the person that mattered most in my life: my mother? But it was time to turn the page. It was time to close that chapter of my life. It was time to push on ahead.

Maybe I could land a good job, start a wonderful career, and let my past be that: my past.

My sister Sandra had a beautiful one-bedroom condo. It was just her and me, so the one-bedroom wasn't bad at all. Plus, I enjoyed sleeping on the floor. I know it may sound weird (my sister didn't get it either), but her bed was too soft. I know; call me odd for choosing the hard floor over a soft bed. I guess I was just different in that way. If the bed was too soft, I could not have a good night's rest. The living-room floor was perfect. And the couch was amazing. It was a win-win for me. Soon after, my sister had to leave on a trip. I didn't mind. It wasn't like I had a say-so if she stayed or went, but I did not mind the alone time I was going to have. I would have a few days to unwind my thoughts, let my feelings run wild, and just kick, scream, and cry if I had to—which I did. My sister left, and I was alone. Perfect. I would just close my eyes and try to rest. The house phone rang. I answered, "Hello?"

"Buzz me up right now. Buzz me up right now," my mother yelled.

You got to be kidding me. Lord have mercy. Why is she even here? God, where is my break? I just want a break. I can't take any more of this.

Hanging up on my mother I quickly called my sister Carmen who lived just about eleven minutes away. I asked her to come over and explained to her that our mother was waiting in the lobby to get buzzed up. She was shocked to hear that our mother was even over here. Not asking a lot of questions, she began to make her way over.

The phone rang again. I answered.

"Hello?"

"Hey, sis. It's me. I have Mom with me. Buzz us up."

I buzzed them up. I was hoping that, by having my sister with me, my mother would be more at ease. *Nope.* Not the case. My mother came in, yelling, "You are *never* going to be anything. You'll be just like your father."

I was in total shock. I was so disappointed in myself. And I didn't even know why. Tears running down my face, I was left to feel like a complete failure. Where had I gone wrong as a child? Where had I gone wrong? My sister interrupted our mother. "Mom, stop. Stop. Why are you speaking to her like that?"

Now my sister was crying. I literally had no idea how I was even standing at this point. I had nothing left in me. And when I thought it was over, it wasn't.

I stood by the door just in case I wanted to leave out and leave them there alone; I watched my mother's body language as she stood in the living room. I could tell something was coming and here it was. These next few words from my mother stung me to the core.

"You are a mistake!" My mother said.

I was yelling within myself. I was inwardly shouting for help. *Lord, why the hard times? Why the tribulations? Why the pain? Why must I take it upon myself to take what others do to me? Lord, I can't. I just can't any longer. Day by day I try. But does it get better? No. You said you'll be with me always, but I feel it's only me walking. Where are you, Lord? Please, where are you? My body is tired of seeking. I might as well give up. I send up praises so that blessings may fall, but all that's fallen is heartache and pain. Please make this pain go away.*

My mother continued, "You are a mistake, and you'll be just like your father: nothing. You are from North Philly, and no good will come out of you. I did not want you. It was your father. It was his idea to keep you. He forced me to carry you. I wanted to get an abortion, but he wanted me to keep you."

My heart dropped. Tears were now flowing uncontrollably. Was this story true? Did my mother not want me? She was just having a bad day, right? If this were true, then it would make so much sense that my daddy would always call me his miracle. I was my mom's mistake and my daddy's miracle. Great. So now I had this to deal with. I just stared at my mother. I had nothing to say. All I wanted was a hug. But I better not move a muscle. My sister Carmen could not take any more of this verbal abuse: "Mom, it's time to go. It's time to go."

As soon as they both left, I fell to the ground. In my own puddle of tears, I heard the Lord say, "Get up. Get up. Here are the answers that you seek. I created and molded you in *my* image. Meaning that everything I do is perfect. You're talking about pain, trails, and tribulation? Abby, did you forget? Did you forget what I did for you? Or where I went for you? Hard times? I took every pain for you. I went through every trial for you, and yet you still say, why? Day by day, you try? It's day by day that I awake you. I pour new grace and mercy into you every morning. You say you can't any longer? Did I hear you correctly? My child, you can't any longer? How is it that you can sit there and say you can't any longer after I told you that you can? You can do all things through Christ who strengthens you. My child, know this: the time will come when you won't have to cry about this any longer. Never think you're walking alone. It's me who's carrying you.

"Never give up my child. I was tired heading to the cross. But I had you in mind the whole time. I pushed my way to the cross because, at the end, I knew we would win. My body was tired of the whips, but I took each one for you. By my stripes, you are healed.

Child, who else did you think you could talk to besides me? I am the beginning and the end. Your life starts and ends with me. The next time you have a *why* question, you ask yourself, 'Why not?' *Now get up, Abby!*"

At that moment, I felt a power rush all over me. I can't really explain it. But I knew my life had meaning. I knew that, if I could just tap into my purpose, I could show my mother I was somebody. I would be somebody. I would not be average. My heart was beating faster than normal. I'd just come in contact with the ruler of the universe. No more would I allow someone to break me. I had been broken enough. Now I pressed toward the mark for the prize of the high calling of God in Christ Jesus (Philippians 3:14). The rocks thrown at me had now cracked open my anointing. I rose with all power in my hand.

"From where does my help come? My help comes from the Lord, who made heaven and earth" (Psalm 121:1–2).

That day, my life had meaning.

My father had already gone back to Puerto Rico, and—you know what?—I was going to follow him. I purchased a one-way ticket and started packing.

"How long you staying?" Elisa asked.

With a big smile on my face, I said, "Three months."

And after that, I would be heading to Spain. I was convinced this was the break I needed.

"Have fun and be safe," she said.

I was packed and heading to the airport. The flight to Puerto Rico was short and peaceful. When I landed, I could feel the heat. Outside, there was a light breeze, and the air was fresh. There was nothing more I wanted to do than to just sit under a tree and sip on a coconut. Here, my mind was free. No tears. No worries. No disappointments. Just the sun beaming on my face. Each day my father asked what I wanted to do, and every day, my answer was the same: nothing. I just wanted to relax and have my great-auntie sit on my lap while she sipped on her coffee.

Adelina; wow, how I miss her so much. Adelina was no spring chicken, if you know what I mean. She was old in age. Although she looked amazing, her age was catching up with her. She had such a free spirit. She had no worries. Each day, her routine was the same; she fixed her coffee, brought in the pots from outside (filled with rainwater from the night before), and sat on my lap. I don't know why we started doing that, but it was fun. We would watch TV (which I couldn't understand, although I tried), then we would go pick oranges. Oh man, she had an orange tree right in her backyard. We used to hit a few branches, and down would come the oranges. She'd have an orange every day. Like clockwork. May she rest in paradise!

Today, I felt like stepping out and going for a walk. The shops and stores were like little holes in the walls. We had to be sure to step all the way inside, or else we would still be in the street. There was a rally taking place. I had started yelling out a chant that I was hearing other people yell when suddenly my father rushed over to me, telling me to hush up. I didn't understand why, so you know I asked. He said I was chanting the wrong name on the wrong side of the street. Oh, that's why people were looking at me strangely. One side of the street had Republicans, and the other side of the street had Democrats. Now I saw why I was getting unpleasant looks. "Let's just go back home," I whispered to my daddy. We headed back, but this time, we crossed the street so I could chant for the right person on the proper side of the street.

We ended up stopping by my auntie's house (my father's sister); she was surprised to see me. The last time I'd seen her was…well never. I'd never met her before. All she knew was we were family. She was so excited and spoke Spanish so quickly that I had to ask her to slow down. My father left me alone with her for about an hour. I asked him not to, since Spanish was not my first language, but all he said was, "That's your aunt. Figure it out." Then he left. I stood there just smiling at her. About three minutes later, a cousin came through the door.

"Hola," I said.

"Hello," he answered back.

I got excited and wanted to test the waters again. I asked him what his name was in Spanish to see if he would respond in perfect English. And guess what; he did. That was that. I hung out with him most of the time, and he was able to translate whatever words I struggled with. My stay in Puerto Rico was a breeze.

EXCERPTS FROM MY PERSONAL JOURNAL

I've had some bad days, but this has been the worst day of my life. Being called a mistake by my mother was worse than being touched and sexually abused as a kid. I would rather go through rape than know I was her mistake. If only she could stop and look at all the good I've done, she could see that what she thought was a mistake is actually a blessing. After my encounter with the Lord, I do feel brand new. I feel like I can live again. There is still pain from those words, and while moving forward is necessary, healing is a different sport. I will move on, but I need the manual for healing. It's like one blow after another. Up to this point, I've had to let a lot of things go. But that's getting old. I'd rather use my energy to heal. Where do I start? Puerto Rico is the best thing that has happened to me. It was the break I needed. Not sure when I'll be returning, but I'm grateful to have been given the opportunity.

Rest well, Titi Adelina.

CHAPTER 11
CERVICAL CANCER

I WAS BACK from all of my traveling, and I felt great! I was ready to start living and enjoying life. I picked up a job at the gym as a personal trainer. It was the best group of people I've ever worked with. I stayed with this organization for five years, and I don't regret a day of it. I had a random conversation with a gym member. She asked if Planned Parenthood was the best option for a checkup. Since I'd never been to this place, I didn't have a legit answer, but I said, "Yes!" I assured her Planned Parenthood was the place to go. Not knowing where I was sending her, I asked her more about the reason for her visit. She went on to say she was now sexually active and just wanting to make sure she was OK. Well, now a light bulb went off in my head. I was also sexually active. Maybe I too should check out this place. I asked my god-sister, Krystal, if she recommended a specific one to visit. She did, so I went to her recommendation. I had gotten a Pap smear and was told to wait a few days for my results. Well, a few days went by, all of my results were negative. A year later, I went in for another checkup. This visit was different. They referred me to a hospital and a specialist. They mentioned my Pap smear was abnormal.

At the doctor's office for another Pap smear, the nurse called in her assistant. Then she called in the doctor. Everything in me became nervous, anxious, and scared. Only one thought was going through my head. I was dying (but I wasn't). The doctor came in, and at this point, it was a little uncomfortable. What was just supposed to be a fifteen-minute procedure now turned into a forty-five-minute procedure, with three pairs of human eyes staring right at me—and not at my face, if you understand a Pap smear. The doctor peeked up and asked about my age. Nineteen, I told him. Then I asked if everything was OK. He didn't answer. Instead, he walked out with the others, giving me a few minutes to dress myself. When they returned, I asked again if everything was OK. In my mind, I was hoping I wasn't pregnant. And thank God that wasn't the case. So what could have been the problem? The doctor looked at me and said because I was nineteen years old. I didn't need a parent's consent, but in the event that I wanted him to speak with them, he would. In my head, I was like, *Listen, doc. What is it? What is happening?* He went on to say that it looked like cervical cancer, but he wouldn't know for sure until they ran some tests with the samples they'd taken from me.

Cervical cancer? What is he talking about? I'm 19 years old. Why would I be dealing with cervical cancer? My mind raced. You can only imagine where my mind went. The man that touched me all of those years—what did he do to me? Having been so young, did he damage me? Did he do this? I had so many unspoken questions. I left the doctor's office so confused; here I was with another situation that I wouldn't tell anyone about. I had gotten so good at holding stuff in, I would show up to work like nothing was happening. Eleven days went by, and I got a call from the doctor.

"Is everything all right?" I asked.

"No, Abigail. We'll need you to come in. You can bring someone if you like. We encourage you to bring a guardian if possible."

"Sure, doc. No problem. When do you need to see me?"

In my mind, I already knew I wasn't bringing anybody with me, and I wasn't even going to tell anybody.

"Ok, doc. In three days. Yes, I can be there. See you at 11:00 a.m."

Soaking my pillow with tears every night was becoming my normal. If it wasn't one thing, it was another. So here I was at the doctor's office again. Doc told me he knew for sure it was cervical cancer. Wanting to just burst out into tears, I held it all together.

I asked, "So what now? What do I do? I'm only nineteen years old."

Doc remained calm and began with, "Well, we could remove your cervix, and that would take care of all of the cancer cells sitting there."

I stared at him in total disbelief.

"Excuse me, doc, I'm nineteen years old. At this point in my life, I don't think I want any children, but what if I change my mind later in life? If you remove my cervix, then I have a zero chance of ever having children."

The doctor looked at me and said, "Abigail, the cancer cells are only on one side of the cervix. We could remove just half of your cervix."

I sat there, just soaking all of this information in.

My next question: "Doc, if you remove half of my cervix, does that give me half the chance of getting pregnant and half the chance of carrying till full term?"

Doc said, "That is exactly right. If we remove just half of your cervix, then that puts you at a fifty–fifty chance of having children and a fifty–fifty chance of carrying to full term."

I sat there in silence. There had to be another way. I asked the doc if, since the cancer cells were just on one side of my cervix, it would be possible to scrape just that one side. Now, in my mind that sounds like the craziest thing to ask. But I was nineteen years old. I had to ask, even if it sounded silly.

Would you know it, to my surprise, he said, "Yes. Yes Abigail. We could scrape the cancer cells off. We could even laser them off, but it doesn't guarantee a full recovery. The cancer cells could actually come back stronger than they are now. Is that something you want to try first?"

With no hesitation, I answered yes. The doctor asked how I would like to get billed. I thought this was an odd time to ask that question, but then again, he was probably thinking money over cervixes. I knew I wouldn't be able to manage this bill. I asked if there were any state grants that would cover the cost. That day, I learned the true meaning of the phrase "There are no dumb questions." The doctor assured me I would get approved if I applied for a few different grants. The nurse assistant guided me through how to apply, and so I did.

I lay back so the scrapping could begin. I felt every tool that they inserted into me. Where was the numbing cream? Where was the Tylenol or something? There was nothing. Tool after tool—I felt each one. Feeling every scrape was dreadful. As I lay there, tears began to run down my face. They asked if I was OK, but I lied and said yes. I wasn't OK But I was becoming numb to pain. I was becoming a master at hiding my discomfort. Surely this was not how I wanted to live. About thirty minutes went by, and I was able to sit up and dress myself. The doctor came back in and indicated they would send what they'd scraped into the lab and contact me in just a few days. In pain, I walked out of that office. Day after day, I kept my cell phone close to the hip, not wanting to miss the call. A little time went by, then the doctor called. I went back to see him. I sat there waiting to hear my results.

"Abigail, it's been confirmed. It's cancer cells for sure."

Right there with no hesitation, I burst out crying. He sent for a counselor. She walked in and began to ask me 101 questions. I had no idea what she was asking me. I just let her speak and nodded my head to just about everything she was saying. But I heard nothing. About fifteen minutes later, I was able to gather myself, and the doctor came back in. He also confirmed that I had been approved with two grants and they were enough to cover a few visits. Thank God.

"First thing's first," the doctor said. "Before we do anything, we are going to check if any other cancer cells returned after we scrapped you last. I was hoping no cancer cells returned, but of course, that was not the outcome."

Not only had they returned, but also the doctor stated they had spread now to both sides of the cervix, and it was now double the amount of cancer cells. The doctor encouraged me to get my cervix removed before the cancer cells worsened, but I was not on board with that decision. I asked if he could do another scrapping, just one more time. He seemed bothered by my request. It did not take him long to respond.

"Abigail, we've tested your cancer cells. We see it spreading. If we continue scrapping, we are just going to weaken your cervix. It's best to remove the entire cervix."

As he continued talking, this is what I heard: "Blah, blah, blah, blah, blah."

Could my life just pause for a minute? Could I catch a break? Could I catch my breath? I mean, I'd just come out of one of the hardest seasons of my life. I was just getting whole again from everything that had happened to me between seven and fifteen. I was just now able to lift up my head with no shame, and now this? *Why?* Doc agreed to do yet another scrapping. I went home feeling defeated.

Later in the day, I heard the Lord whisper, "Why not?" I fell on my face. Crying before the Lord, I shouted back, "Why not? Why not? Because I just need a break. As if my childhood wasn't enough. I just need a break."

I cried by myself that entire day. My relationship with the Lord had gotten stronger over the years. I knew I loved Him, and I knew I trusted Him, and I didn't doubt Him; I just needed a break. I pleaded with the Lord like never before. I prayed. I fasted. For almost *two* whole years (yes, *two* whole years), I was going in and out of the doctor's office. Until one visit changed everything.

"Abigail, your grant money is gone. There is nothing else left to apply for."

As I listened to those words, something in me rose up. The Lord whispered, "Apply pressure." I asked to be alone in the room for a minute. Sinking in my chair, I asked the Lord what to do now. He said again, "Apply pressure."

"Pressure where? Pressure with whom? God, please I'm begging, heal me. There's no more grant money. Time has run out. If you don't heal me now, I'm done."

Again, I heard the Lord say, "Apply pressure." Then it clicked. I needed to apply pressure to my faith. I stood up. I walked over to the window. I looked up and I said, "Lord, if I never have children, I'll be OK with that. Just please heal me. This is all I have left in me.

I'm tired, and I'm weak." And in that moment, I heard the Lord say, "I am strong. Now apply pressure."

The doctor knocked on the door and then came in. Applying pressure, I said, "Doc, scrape one more time. Just check one more time."

He seemed bothered. "Abigail this been going on for over a year. Almost two."

Remembering what the Lord said, I applied more pressure. "I know, doc. I know. This time, it's different. Just one more time. Please, one more time."

He agreed. I lay back. The doctor asked me to give him a minute as he stepped out of the room. He resumed with the nurse. She looked, then they both left and returned with someone else. Then he looked. They all looked. Then the doc said, "I don't understand."

At *that* moment, I knew that God had healed me. I felt it. I sensed it. I believed it. I applied the pressure to my faith.

The doc said, "I don't understand, Abigail; there is no evidence of you ever having cervical cancer. We have sample cells that we removed from your cervix, but now we can't even detect where we could have gotten the samples. Wait here a minute."

They all left. As soon as that door shut, I burst into tears. "God, thank you. Thank you. Thank you. The doctor may not understand what just happened. But I know. I know it was the pressure of my faith that changed the situation for me."

I went back to the window. I looked up, and with tears in my eyes, I said, "Lord, thank you."

I heard a knock on the door, so I went back to the bed and lay down. I wiped my face, and with a smile, I waited to hear what they had to say. Awestruck, the doctor said, "They weren't too sure what just happened." He said there was nothing.

Not able to contain myself any longer, I shouted, "I know what just happened." I said, "I'm healed because I applied pressure to my faith. God did this. God did this. God did this."

They all smiled as they wiped the tears from their faces.

The doctor said, "Abigail, come back in six months, OK?"

And for two years, I had to show up every six months. After a year, I left Philly and moved to San Diego, California, but every six months, I made my appointment in San Diego, until I was told I no longer had to come every six months. And since then I've never had an abnormal Pap smear. All glory and honor go to the true and living God.

EXCERPTS FROM MY PERSONAL JOURNAL

Pressure. Each letter in that word (PRESSURE) means something to me.

P: Pray

R: Release

E: Exhale

S: Sing

S: Shout

U: Uncommon

R: Reverence

E: Everlasting

I held on to each of these words. I held on to prayer, even when I didn't feel heard. Once I had made up my mind about giving it over to the Lord, I released it all and never looked back. I exhaled, I sang, I shouted, and I gave all glory to God. I knew I was uncommon. I was cut from a different cloth. Because of that, I honored and reverenced the Lord. I knew Him as my everlasting savior. These words are forever in my heart. I've learned such a valuable lesson in the doctor's office. I learned that, if we apply pressure to our faith, we'd see God do the impossible. If we apply pressure to our situation, we'll see God work wonders. If we apply pressure to our faith, He'll open up the windows of heaven. If we apply pressure, He'll allow us to see things that no eyes have seen and no ears have heard.

I learned that applying pressure takes participation from both parties. It takes participation on my end to believe that, if I apply the pressure, then the Lord will release the blessing. It's a two-way street. Nothing changed until I applied pressure to my faith. Someday, somewhere, someone will read this. May my words be an encouragement to you: Apply pressure! If you are waiting for a miracle or a breakthrough, stop crying and worrying; apply pressure to your faith. Begin decreeing and declaring. Begin to speak healing over yourself. In this season, I've learned that no one has the last say but the Lord. It did not matter how the doctor felt about the situation; it was up to me to take heed of what the Lord told me. And as a result, I am healed.

CHAPTER 12

TRUTH NOW TOLD

IT'S 2020, AND as I sit to write this book, I realize that I have so many unanswered questions. At this point in my life, I want and need answers. Not knowing how it would all play out, I took one of my biggest risks and faced my fears. I called my mother to ask her a few questions.

"Hi, Mom. Do you have a minute? I would like to ask you a few questions, if that's OK."

My heart was now pounding. I knew that God had not given me the spirit of fear but of power, of love, and of a sound mind. But right now, if I was honest, I was nervous and a little terrified. My mother was open to hearing my questions, so I opened up with this:

"Mom, tell me about the fall."

After I gave her more details, my mother began.

"You were in the house sitting in your walker. You then began to walk throughout the house when suddenly I heard a loud noise and your sister screaming. It was you falling down the basement steps in your baby walker. Till this day, I have no idea how the basement door got open. I was in the kitchen cooking. All I know is that when I went to check on you, you was absolutely fine. You had no scratches, no bumps or bruises. You were sitting on the bottom step while your walker was against the wall. I believe the angel of the Lord was with you."

Finished with that topic I drank some water, told myself that was easy, and moved on to a more sensitive topic. Hoping she wouldn't shut down, I went for it.

"Mom, why didn't you believe me?"

Silence now taking over, I asked again, "Mom, why didn't you believe me?"

My mother was not following; she needed me to fill in some blanks. I'd been hoping I wouldn't have to do that. Trying to hold all of my emotions together, I went forward with, "Mom, when I was telling you that man was touching me, why didn't you believe me? Why did you continue allowing him to come around?"

Silence. I didn't want to break the silence this time. I figured I'd give my mother time to catch her breath, maybe even gather her thoughts. Then she spoke: "I don't know. You were so young, I didn't think he was really doing those things to you."

As my mother spoke, I realized that I was in a different place spiritually and mentally, and forgave her. Then she told me something that just about blew me away.

She said, "Abby, I should have believed you. One day, when he brought you back home from taking you to McDonalds, he told me that one day you would be his."

On the phone with my mouth wide open and not thinking straight, I interrupted my mother and said, "Mom, he said that to you, and you still didn't believe me?"

Quickly, I apologized for the outburst and asked her to finish with her thought.

"To answer your question," she continued, "that statement did not sit well with me. I told you to get in the house and asked him to leave. He drove off, and I told him then not to come around for a while. But after a while, I allowed him to come back around, and I really don't know why. I was just busy being a single mom, trying to raise six children while finishing nursing school. I should have paid more attention to you. I should have paid more attention to all of you."

Now wanting to go deeper, I said, "Mom, you kicked me out of the house on my prom night. You embarrassed me outside in front of all of my family and friends. Why? What did I do to make you so angry with me? I was a great student. I played almost every sport. I made the National Honor Society. I was a White William Scholar. I was senior class president. I made the top twenty-five-student list. Why the embarrassment on that night?"

"Abby, I thought you were up to something. A few weeks before prom, some guys came to the house. They said the guy you were currently dating at that time was a bad guy and you turned those guys down from being a potential prom date because you were going to have this 'dangerous' guy waiting for you at the prom."

OK, at this point in the conversation I became so confused. But I stayed quiet until she finished.

She continued, "And you taking your sister Elisa to your prom—I thought that was the cover up."

She stopped talking, and then I began. "Mom, please let me get this straight. I got kicked out of the house because some strangers who you cannot name came to the house and told you a bunch of lies that you never questioned or asked me about? Is that right?"

My mother continued, "Yes. That's right. And this guy that you supposedly had been dating—I had never seen or met him before, so I thought they were telling the truth. I thought, since you never brought him around, I figured he was as dangerous as they were saying he was."

"Mom, he was in the navy. That's why you haven't met him. Once he graduated, he went straight to the military. That was my reason for taking my sister to prom. I didn't want to take any other guy. I believed who I chose to take to my prom should have been my decision. Sure, there were plenty of guys that asked for me to be their prom date, but I did say no. But how was that wrong of me? The guy I was currently dating could not come home in time to join me. I wasn't covering anything up. Is there more to this story that I should know about? Because this really doesn't make any sense."

Silence.

My mother apologized. She didn't speak on anything that I'd just said; she just apologized. Lord knows, I accepted her apology. But something in me just felt like I'd lost out on enjoying my prom night, all because of a lie. I got kicked out of my mother's house on prom night all because of a lie. This story wasn't adding up. But I wasn't going to force it. I figured, if I was going to get the whole truth, then it would be now. And if I didn't get the whole truth now, then I would never get the truth.

I had struggled with the final question for years because I wasn't sure if I truly wanted an answer. But I went for it.

"Mom, you told me on multiple occasions that I was an accident and a mistake. Is that the truth, or were you speaking out of anger?"

My heart stopped beating. I didn't know how this would turn out. With no hesitation, she answered, "I did not want you, Abby. And I thought you would never ask me this question."

Suddenly, I was fighting back my tears, my soul was screaming "Why, Mom? Why?" I remained quiet. Then she continued.

"I had four children already, Abby. I was a single mother of four. I did not want any more children. It was your father who wanted ten children. I found out I was pregnant with you when I was three months pregnant—or I thought I was three months pregnant. I went to see my doctor and asked for an abortion then. But they couldn't do it. I wasn't three months pregnant. I was five months pregnant. I was angry the entire pregnancy. I cursed my stomach. I wished your death. And most importantly, I was more upset that I even got pregnant when my tubes were tied. My doctor guaranteed me seven years of my tubes being tied. It was just a little over two years when I became pregnant with you. I'm sorry, but I meant that when I said it. You were a mistake."

"But how do you feel now, Mom? How do you feel now? After all I've accomplished and achieved on my own, how do you feel about me now?"

As I waited for my mother to respond, I felt mixed emotions. Half of me was becoming angry, and the other half of me was remaining humble. Here I was, putting myself on the edge of a cliff to either get pushed over or saved by what my mother would say next. I waited to hear her response. After a moment of silence, I asked again, "How do you feel about me now? I really need to know."

"Abigail, I am satisfied. People told me when I was pregnant with you that this pregnancy would be a blessing. Not to say that none of my other pregnancies wasn't a blessing, because all of my children are a blessing—but it was something about you. And although people told me over and over again that this pregnancy would be a blessing, I was in no state of mine to receive that. As a matter of fact, I didn't receive it. I wanted out of this pregnancy. But now, Abigail, yes! I am proud of you. Hearing all that you've gone through since you were seven years old and hearing how you still were able to maintain good grades, join after-school activities, and remain strong is mind blowing.

"I had no idea you were struggling so much. I can't go back and change what has been said and done, but I can move forward. I'm sorry. I am so sorry that I continued to have him pick you up. I had no idea. I never thought to stop what I was doing to communicate with you, because I really didn't know how to communicate. My mother never communicated well with me. So all I knew to do was work. I had six children to feed. But I'm so proud of you, daughter. I can't take credit for anything you've accomplished. You moved out of Philly on your own and moved to California for eight years. You brought yourself back to Philly for a few months before getting married and moving to Ohio. You did that. I'm sorry you did it alone. I'm learning now how to communicate, and I ask that you forgive me, daughter. I ask that you accept my apology."

As I sat on the phone and listened to my mother, I could feel her pain. I could feel the regret. As she continued to speak, I purposely said nothing. I just wiped the tears that had fallen as she continued to speak to me. I don't know what was more exciting to me—the fact that I had my mother on the phone for over an hour (never happened) or the fact that she was apologizing. Either way, I was satisfied. My heart was full. I was on cloud nine. But then I suddenly snapped out of it when I heard my mother say, "I can tell you more face to face."

I had to quickly respond. Knowing that I was in Ohio and she was in Philly, there was no telling the next time I would be able to get down there.

"Mom, let's keep going. I need to hear everything you have to say. This book will be published this year. I can't wait to finish writing. There's no telling when I'm going to see you, especially with this pandemic."

My response caught my mother by surprise. "Abigail, this year, 2020—you want to publish this year, but you've only been writing for four months."

I assured her I was only making this a six-month project. I was going to write and publish my book in six months. I assured her I was serious about moving forward. I was serious about telling my story and letting it be heard. I was ready to release this pain I'd been holding on to for years and to let it work for my good. No longer would I be held back by a seven-year-old mindset in a thirty-four-year-old body. This book was happening this year, 2020.

My mother, now excited, continued talking: "So, as I was saying, I am very proud of you. And I do look forward to seeing what more comes out of you. I know this is just the beginning for you. When you set your mind to do something, one thing I know about you, daughter, is that you will get it done and succeed."

I thanked my mother from the bottom of my heart; I assured her that I would carry the scripture in my heart that told me to "Honor your father and your mother, that your days may be long in the land that the Lord your God is giving you" (Exodus 20:12 [ESV]).

I told my mother that, if I desired everything I touched to be blessed, the one thing I could not do was dishonor her. I always kept that in the forefront of my mind. I took this time to ask my mother for forgiveness. Though anger had grown in my heart when I was a child and resentment had become my BFF, I wanted her to know that I had grown out of that. I explained that, at times, I knew I was rude intentionally. I knew I had a strong attitude. And so many people judged me for the attitude I carried and that just made matters worse for me because they had no idea where it came from. I shared with my mother that no one knew where my hate for men started and why. I shared with her that not one friend ever knew I was being touched in places that I should never have experienced at the age of seven. But in all of that, I told my mother that I was sorry. I asked for her forgiveness and a chance to work toward a better and healthier relationship.

My mother explained how she would love to move forward and build a better and healthier relationship with me. She also accepted my apology. Before we ended the conversation, I wanted to just ask one final question. I went for it:

"Mom, since we're talking, after you kicked me out of the house, was it really necessary to not allow me in the house when I wanted to visit MyYaya (my little sister Rebecca)? You had me wait outside every time I came to visit her, and you didn't allow me in to use the bathroom when needed. What that necessary?"

With laughter, my mother said she was sorry and that none of that was necessary. Still laughing, she said she should have let me in, especially on those days when I needed to use the restroom. Since my mother was having a real kick out of this, it also made me laugh. It felt good to have had this conversation.

EXCERPTS FROM MY PERSONAL JOURNAL

Well, you did it, Abby. All of your unspoken truths are now told. I thought there would have been more said concerning "the man," but there wasn't. I thought maybe she would have asked questions about what he did and when, where and how, but she didn't. Maybe for her own sanity, she didn't want to know. And that's OK. I didn't want to volunteer all of what happened to me. I figured, if her heart could take it, she would ask. But if she reads this book, she'll definitely know. I left nothing out. There was our house, his car, and his basement—all told. After writing and publishing this book, I will still be open if she wants to ask or say more.

CHAPTER 13
ALL THINGS POSSIBLE

AS I SIT here as my thirty-four-year-old self, I think about all of the pauses I had in my life, the first pause beginning at just seven years old. This pause was the deadliest. Who knew it would last for almost eight years. I am left to think about the many times I tried to press "play" in my life, only to have God turn around and hit the pause button. What was He saying? What was the message? What was the lesson?

I realize God planted me not where it would be easy, but where I was called. I did not know why; I could not put my finger on it, but now I see. Now I know that it was all for my good. It was all for this book. It was all for the next young boy or girl who finds himself or herself being touched in unwanted places. No matter how I feel about it, it was all for my good. I see now that God used my pain to form me. He used my pain to break me out of my comfort zone. He used my pain so I could do this: stand and declare the goodness of the Lord. As I think on those things, I look back in total amazement.

Had God stopped it back then when I was seven years old, I would not have this message today. I would not have learned the lesson. The lesson was to prove to me that He would do just what

He said; He would never leave me nor forsake me. The lesson was to prove Himself as Alpha and Omega, the beginning and the end. The lesson was to show that *all* things work together for the good to those who love Him, who have been called according to His purpose (Romans 8:28). I stand here writing to you today, shouting from the roof top, "Father, Jehovah, I love you. I trust you. And I honor you."

I take this moment to speak into the life of every young boy and girl. No matter where you are, no matter how deep in pain you may be, God is still in control, and He takes His seat at the throne. He has you in the palm of His hand. He hasn't forgotten about you. Every morning that He awakes you, He's calling on you to make it. He's calling on you to trust Him just a little bit more. He trusts you not to give up. He's trusting you to believe in the scripture that says, "Greater is He that is in you than he who is in the world" (1 John 4:4 [ESV]). Hold on, young boy; hold on, young girl; you don't have to be a victim. You do have a voice. You can change the narrative. You can speak up. And I'm here for it. You are not alone and will never be alone. Our Heavenly Father, who holds the entire universe in the palm of His hand, cares for you. He hasn't lost sight of you. He said in His Word, "Come to Me all that are tired, all that are burnt out," and He promises He will give you rest (Matthew 11:28). So, child, you can stop running now. You can stop crying yourself to sleep. You can lift up your head. You can place your crown back in its rightful place. You can free yourself, and you can do it today. With God, all things are possible.

If you are reading this book, just know that this is just my beginning. This is just the experience that God used to crack my anointing open. So now, I walk by faith and not by sight. Now I walk victoriously. With my head held high. Now I know that I am royalty. And the reason the enemy could not take me out as a child was that my anointing and my protection had gone out before me, long before we even met. The Lord saw fit to now press the play button in my life, because I'm ready. I'm ready to speak up. I'm ready to tell my story. I'm ready to move on. I'm ready to become the woman that He created and molded me to be when He formed me in my mother's womb. He pressed play because I've matured. He pressed play because the work that He started in me will now be accomplished. And while I am at it, let me just say that it does not matter who wants to give an opinion. The fact of the matter is, I was taken to a place where He knew it would not be easy but it would be worth it.

And it has all been worth it!

God had to remind me of Jeremiah 29:11 (ESV): "For I know the plans I have for you, declares the Lord, plans for welfare and not for evil, to give you a future and a hope."

So while all hell was breaking loose in my life, God with His loving arms, continued to look down on me and tell me, "But I got you. Abby, if you just go through one more thing for my name's sake, I promise you, you'll see the salvation of the Lord."

I stand here today, proud of myself. I no longer want better for my life. No, that's the minimum. Now I want the promise. I want everything God has ever promised me. And slowly God is giving me His promises. He has given me the husband who can water my bed sheets. Oh, for that I'm grateful. He has given me the man who can take my pain and peal back the layers one at a time. He has given me the man who can identity my hurts and pain and cover them with his love. I am no longer dragging old habits and going down memory lane. No, those days are over. My chains have been broken, and I've been released to tell the world that, if you just hold on to God's unchanging hand, it doesn't matter if you can't see the light at the end of the tunnel. The fact that *He is* the light is enough to keep you going, and it is enough to ensure that no weapons formed against you shall prosper (Isaiah 54:17).

APPLY PRESSURE

If there is anything I can leave you with, it's this: apply pressure to your faith. If you are waiting on a miracle, apply pressure. If you are waiting for a breakthrough, apply pressure. If you are waiting for God to make ways out of no ways, apply pressure. My healing did not happen until I totally surrendered the situation to the Lord. I was busy trying to hold on to my cervix when God was saying to release it to Him and He would heal me. My God. I stand healed today because I learned the value of pressure. Often times, when the pressure is on us, we look for a way out. We look for someone to spot us. And God is saying, "Stop looking for somebody to spot you. I am your spotter. I will lift the weight off of you when the pressure gets too heavy."

I know all about weights and needing a spotter. As a twelve-year personal trainer, I know what it means in the natural to need a spotter. I know what it means in the natural to need someone stronger than me to take the weight off me. I know what it means in the natural to learn the posture for working out. You cannot just go to the gym, pick up any weight, and lift it any way. There is a way you have to bend your knees if you want to squat. There is a way you must position your back if you want to bench press. There is a way to position your shoulders for back-flyers.

So, if there's a natural stance we must take when lifting the natural weight, then there's also a spiritual stance we must take when we are lifting in the supernatural. The position is this: down on your knees with your hands lifted up. That's the position that yells, "Spot me, Jesus!" I know all too well how, when both hands are lifted up, it sounds the alarm in heaven. I know all too well that, when a tear begins to form itself, the Holy Spirit catches it before it falls, because no tears ever go to waste. And we know this because Psalm 56:8 says that our tears are placed in a bottle. He sees and He knows all things. From our first newborn cries to the tears we shed as children, to the adolescent years of puberty, to the anxiety of adulthood, and even to the complication of old age. Every tear, every cry, every burden, and every hurtful moment—He's seen it all. And now He is wiping the slate clean. Your new beginning and my new beginning start here. Start now.

LET ME PRAY FOR YOU

Father, I just want to take this time to thank you for each reader. I pray, Father, that you use this book to set each one free from whatever may have them in bondage. Whether its sexual, physical, or verbal abuse. I pray, Father, that you help to set them free. Father, you have come so that we may have life and have it abundantly. I lift up each reader to you now, Father. I declare healing over them and new beginnings. I pray strategies over their lives, strategies to beat the enemy when he comes with his lies. They will no longer be victims. The enemy cannot have them. We take back our children, teenagers, young adults, and adults. We give them to you, Father. We rebuke any and everyone who wants to come into their lives to destroy them.

We know that no weapons formed against them shall prosper. Lord, they will not be touched. They will not be raped. They will not be violated. They shall keep their innocence. They shall not have to live before their time. They shall be respected. They shall be heard. They shall be honored, and they too shall give honor to You. We cover these babies in prayer, Father. And we cover adults the same way. No more slave trafficking. No more sexual abuse. No more cocaine to feel the void. No more alcohol to drain the pain. No more, Father. We call on you, great God. Fill the void, Lord. Cover, protect, and heal this land.

In Jesus' precious name, amen.

Praise for *Elite Capture*

"I was waiting for this book without realizing I was waiting for this book." —**Ruth Wilson Gilmore**, author of *Change Everything: Racial Capitalism* and the *Case for Abolition*

"Olúfẹ́mi O. Táíwò is a thinker on fire. He not only calls out empire for shrouding its bloodied hands in the cloth of magical thinking but calls on all of us to do the same. Elite capture, after all, is about turning oppression and its cure into a (neo)liberal commodity exchange where identities become capitalism's latest currency rather than the grounds for revolutionary transformation. The lesson is clear: only when we think for ourselves and act with each other, together in deep, dynamic, and difficult solidarity, can we begin to remake the world." —**Robin D. G. Kelley**, author of *Freedom Dreams: The Black Radical Imagination*

"Olúfẹ́mi O. Táíwò's book is worth sitting with and absorbing. While critically examining what happens when elites hijack our critiques and terminologies for their own interests, *Elite Capture* acutely reminds us that building power globally means we think and build outside of our internal confines. That is when we have the greatest possibility at worldmaking." —**Ibram X. Kendi**, National Book Award–winning author of *Stamped from the Beginning* and *How to Be an Antiracist*

"Olúfẹ́mi O. Táíwò offers an indispensable and urgent set of analyses, interventions, and alternatives to "identity politics," "centering," and much more. The book offers a sober assessment of the state of our racial politics and a powerful path on how to build the world that we deserve." —**Derecka Purnell**, author of *Becoming Abolitionists*

"With global breadth, clarity, and precision, Olúfẹ́mi O. Táíwò dissects the causes and consequences of elite capture and charts an alternative constructive politics for our time. The result is an erudite yet accessible book that draws widely on the rich traditions of black and anti-colonial political thought." **—Adom Getachew**, author of *Worldmaking after Empire: The Rise and Fall of Self-Determination*

"Among the churn of books on 'wokeness' and 'political correctness,' philosopher Olúfẹ́mi O. Táíwò's *Elite Capture* clearly stands out. With calm, clarity, erudition, and authority, Táíwò walks the reader through the morass, deftly explicating the distinction between substantive and worthy critique and weaponized backlash. Understanding the culture wars is essential to US politics right now, and no one has done it better than Táíwò in this book." **—Jason Stanley**, author of *How Fascism Works*

"Olúfẹ́mi O. Táíwò is one of the great social theorists of our generation. *Elite Capture* is a brilliant, devastating book. Táíwò deploys his characteristic blend of philosophical rigor, sociological insight, and political clarity to reset the debate on identity politics. Táíwò shows how the structure of racial capitalism, not misguided activism, is today's prime threat to egalitarian, antiracist politics. And Táíwò's suggested path forward, a constructive and materialist politics at the radical edge of the possible, is exactly what we need to escape these desperate times. Anyone concerned with dismantling inequalities and building a better world needs to read this book." **—Daniel Aldana Cohen**, coauthor of *A Planet to Win: Why We Need a Green New Deal*

"Táíwò's book is an insightful and fascinating look at how it is that elites capture and subvert efforts to better society. Anyone who wants to understand and improve upon the activist movements shaking our world needs to read this book." **—Liam Kofi Bright**, assistant professor at the London School of Economics

"This book, building on one of the most lucid, powerful, and important essays I can recall reading in recent years, is, in a word, brilliant. Read it—and read it twice. Every sentence contains multitudes." **—Daniel Denvir**, host of *The Dig*

Elite
Capture

How the Powerful
Took Over Identity Politics
(and Everything Else)

Olúfẹ́mi O. Táíwò

Haymarket Books
Chicago, Illinois

Published in 2022 by
Haymarket Books
P.O. Box 180165
Chicago, IL 60618
773-583-7884
www.haymarketbooks.org
info@haymarketbooks.org

ISBN: 978-1-64259-735-6

Distributed to the trade in the US through Consortium Book Sales
and Distribution (www.cbsd.com) and internationally through
Ingram Publisher Services International
(www.ingramcontent.com).

This book was published with the generous support of Lannan
Foundation and Wallace Action Fund.

Special discounts are available for bulk purchases by organizations
and institutions. Please email info@haymarketbooks.org for more
information.

Cover design by Steve Leard.

Printed in the United States.

Library of Congress Cataloging-in-Publication data is available.

Contents

Acknowledgments

As always, I have an uncountable number of people to thank for this work.

Thanks to my family for their support: my siblings Ibukun and Ebun, and my parents Abiola and Yetunde, all the Taiwos and Sokunbis, and all the Cincinnati Nigerians; Abigail Higgins, the Higginses, and the Kennedys.

I'd like to thank my editor, Emma Young, and Haymarket's, Sam Smith, as well as all those who helped make the logistics of this book possible: Anthony Arnove, Stephanie Steiker, Suzanne Lipinska and those at KIOSK and Africasia who made her journalistic work available to me, including Simon Delobel and Mathieu Kleyebe Abonnenc. This book grew out of two essays published at *Boston Review* and *The Philosopher*. I want to thank Deb Chasman, Matt Lord, and their colleagues at *Boston*, as well as Chiara Ricciardone and Anthony Morgan and their colleagues at *The Philosopher* for their support on the initial versions of this idea, which made this book possible.

A special thanks to supportive scholars whose direct and indirect support made it possible for me to be here at all: AJ Julius, Daniela Dover, Melvin Rogers, Jason Stanley, Gaye Theresa Johnson, and folks whose work, teaching, or leadership I leaned on implicitly or explicitly: Josh Armstrong, Quill Kukla, Mark Lance, Bryce Huebner, Henry Richardson. To friends and comrades whose support and advice was were just as essential to making it through the writing: Liam Kofi Bright, Marques Vestal, Thabisile Griffin, Austin Branion, Alexis Cooke, Shelbi Nahwilet Meissner, Joel Michael "Boxcutter Joelie" Reynolds, Jeanne-Marie Jackson-Awotwi.

To the institutions and organizations I have able to learn in and from: The Undercommons, UAW 2865, UCLA Labor Center, LA Black Workers Center, and Pan-African Community Action.

To our moral ancestors, without whose struggle and sacrifice none of this would be possible: to the anti-colonial fighters, to the abolitionists, to the workers who demanded more, and to the activists who refused to accept less.

To all of our moral and genealogical descendants, to those who are yet young and those who are yet to come: with love, with hope, and with solidarity.

Introduction

"There is no racism, no tribalism; we are not struggling merely so that we may have a flag, an anthem and ministers. We are not going to install ourselves in the Governors' palace, that is not our objective. . . . We are struggling to liberate our people not only from colonialism but also from any form of exploitation.

We want no one to exploit our people any more, neither whites nor blacks."

—Amílcar Cabral, *Unity and Struggle*[1]

The beginning of the pandemic lockdowns in the spring of 2020 announced lulls in much of business as usual: public transportation, interstate travel, nightlife, community programming, libraries, barbershops. Even playgrounds went silent. But it did not stop police murders around the globe.

In some cases, the lockdowns even set the killings into motion: on March 31, four days after Kenya's curfew began, Kenyan police officers enforced the order by storming a neighborhood and beating people indiscriminately, eventually opening fire with live ammunition.[2] One of these bullets struck and killed Yasin Hussein Moyo, a thirteen-year-old looking down onto the fracas from his apartment balcony. On May 19, twenty-one-year-old Anderson Arboleda was chased by two police officers in Puerto Tejada, Colombia, for breaking pandemic curfew. He was beaten and pepper-sprayed so severely that he died the next morning.[3]

In other cases, the pandemic simply failed to sufficiently disrupt the normal patterns of police violence: on May 18, three police officers entered a home in Rio de Janeiro's Complexo do Salgueiro favela where six cousins were playing together.[4] They opened fire, shooting fourteen-year-old João Pedro Matos Pinto in the back. A relative drove him to a police helicopter in a desperate attempt to get him medical care. The family knew neither his whereabouts nor his medical condition until seventeen hours later—when they found his body at the coroner. By Rio de Janeiro police's own estimates, they killed an average of six people per day in early 2020; if these killings followed the pattern of the past decade, more than three quarters of the dead were Black men.[5] For a sense of scale: there were nearly twice as many police killings in the single Brazilian state of Rio de Janeiro in 2019 as there were across the entire United States in that same year.[6]

In the United States, a spate of police killings whose victims included Breonna Taylor (March 13), George Floyd (May 25), and Tony McDade (May 27) launched a volume of protest unprecedented in US history: by some estimates, as many as twenty-six million people in the country participated in one form or another, a figure that would represent nearly 8 percent of the entire US population.[7] The protests were not only large, but combative. Across the country, luxury malls and retail stores were sacked and pillaged. In Minneapolis, police fled the Third Precinct for their lives as rebels smashed windshields with projectiles and set the building on fire.

The protests were global in scope. In June 2020, demonstrators took to the streets in cities across the world, including Rio, Seoul, London, Sydney, and Monrovia.[8] This global solidarity undoubtedly owes itself to the steadfast international organizing work of Black Lives Matter chapters, the umbrella Movement for Black Lives, and a number of other organizations around the world working in partnership and solidarity with them. But it also is rooted in the global nature of the intersecting dynamics of racism and policing. These problems are among the many legacies of our immediate past that shape our lives today.

In Nigeria, the energy crested a few months later, in October 2020, when protestors took to the streets to call for the abolition of the country's Special Anti-robbery Squad (SARS), a secretive police force that has been responsible for waves of extrajudicial torture, sexual assault, and murder of Nigerians. The #EndSARS protestors were met with bitter resistance—and live ammunition—from the Nigerian government, including during the infamous Lekki Toll Gate massacre. Amnesty International put the death toll at twelve.[9] It is important to understand that the #EndSARS protesters were not merely sympathetic to, or influenced by, other protests earlier in the year, but were fighting on their own front in the same struggle.

Nigeria's Special Anti-robbery Squad, US police forces, and many other repressive bodies use similar ideological

structures and strategies of violence because they are similar kinds of institutions, created to achieve similar aims.
Most of these forces have their roots in the colonial era of
the nineteenth and twentieth centuries, when national-level
institutions functioned like franchises under the global racial
empire's logo, each territorial army, colonial government, and
national stock exchange linked together in a powerful cartel.
While individual security forces were dedicated to different
national interests under the global racial empire, the cartel as
a whole served the interests of the same elites, making sure
wealth and advantage flowed south to north, Black to white.
That system has never been dismantled. So, while "empire"
is no longer a popular term in global politics, we're still ba-
sically living it: nakedly imperial structures live on in forms
like France's management of currencies of many of its former
African colonies, and seemingly neutral international corporations and institutions bully the poorer peoples and countries
of the world in "neocolonial" fashion.[10]

So, despite differences in local context, when people
around the world rose up against the police terror and violence to which they have been subjected for hundreds of
years, it was immediately clear that something global was at
stake. The response from governing elites was equally immediate: the World Bank established a "Task Force on Racism,"
and the United Nations, under pressure from the entire African Union bloc of fifty-four countries, agreed to launch a
yearlong inquiry into anti-Black racism.[11]

Two strategic trends in the response quickly became clear:
the elites' tactic of performing symbolic identity politics to

pacify protestors without enacting material reforms; and their efforts to rebrand (not replace) existing institutions, also using elements of identity politics.

In a stunningly clear summary of the first trend, the mayor of Washington, DC, had "Black Lives Matter" painted on streets near the White House, atop which protestors continued to be brutalized. The following year, the Central Intelligence Agency rolled out the second strategy, producing a dozen "Humans of CIA" recruitment videos reaching out to multiple identity groups, including queer and Indigenous people. Journalist Roberto Lovato cautioned readers about the resonance of this moment in an aptly titled article, "The Age of Intersectional Empire Is Upon Us": "In the vast world that lives outside of progressive circles, there are millions of people who have emotional reactions to Army and Marine recruitment ads featuring proud Black and Latinx soldiers."[12]

Formal political task forces, encouraging murals, and inspirational commercials are serviceable carrots. But there's also, of course, the stick. By June 2021, twenty-five state legislatures had introduced legislation to ban the teaching of "critical race theory," as part of a culture war backed by think tanks such as the Heritage Foundation and Manhattan Institute, alongside well-connected individuals such as Mark Meadows (a former White House chief of staff in the Trump administration).[13] In the United Kingdom, the British government formed a Commission on Race and Ethnic Disparities, which released a report exonerating the government of the institutional racism alleged by Black Lives Matter protestors.[14] Where co-optation fails, regular old repression will do.

So what, then, are we to make of identity politics? Some expressions of identity politics are twisted to rebrand old imperial projects, while others are actively banned by the powers that be. Is it itself an innocuously different version of left politics, separated from more orthodox left politics mainly by "failures of communication" as philosopher Ashley Bohrer suggests?[15] Or, more ominously, is identity politics "an essential tool utilized by the bourgeoisie to maintain its class domination over the working class by keeping workers divided along racial and gender lines," as Dominic Gustavo alleges at the *World Socialist Web Site*?[16] Or is identity politics, as embodied in critical race theory, a dangerous ideology and threat to the established order that the powers that be aim to stamp out?

The Combahee River Collective (and Why Identity Politics Isn't What You Think It Is)

The term "identity politics" was first popularized by the 1977 manifesto of the Combahee River Collective, an organization of queer, Black feminist socialists, and it was supposed to be about fostering solidarity and collaboration.

American studies scholar Duchess Harris recounts the collective's origin story as follows: in 1961, President John F. Kennedy convened a Commission on the Status of Women. It was split into four consultative bodies, one of which was the Consultation on Negro Women. This event inspired sequels, and the third National Conference of Commissions on the Status of Women birthed the meeting that founded the National Organization for Women, which founders hoped would serve as an "NAACP for women." However, NOW failed to live up to this promise to treat race seriously—and Black nationalist organizations failed equally to address gender.[17] As a result, in 1973, activists formed the National Black Feminist Organization.[18]

In 1974, the young activist Barbara Smith met Demita Frazier after she began organizing an NBFO chapter in Boston. The pair agreed with many NBFO goals but also wanted an organization that would discuss "radical economics" more freely and that would guarantee a voice for lesbians. And so, from a meeting of four, began the Combahee River Collective. From 1977 to 1980, they held seven retreats with fellow activists, which were attended by like-minded Boston veteran activists, and even the famed writer Audre Lorde.

The experiences that united these activists—the consistent sidelining and devaluation of their political priorities within different political organizations—were foundational to the stance they developed, which they christened "identity politics."

"We, as black women, we actually had a right to create political priorities and agendas and actions and solutions based in our experiences," Smith later explained—a political agenda based in their full experiences and interests, rather than positioning them as white women's tokens or as Black men's secretaries, and one that incorporated the full complexity of their values, rather than a degraded and misshapen caricature of them. As Princeton professor Keeanga-Yamahtta Taylor puts it, "One could not expect Black women to be wholly active in political movements that neither represented nor advanced their interests"; therefore, the identity politics they developed served as "*entry points* for Black women to engage in politics," rather than a whole cloth withdrawal from problematic organizations and movements.[19]

As such, they were in favor of diverse coalitional organizing, an approach that Smith later saw exemplified by the Bernie Sanders presidential campaign's grassroots approach and its focus on social issues that people of many identities face, especially "basic needs of food, housing and healthcare."[20] Beverly Smith, another of the group's founders, recalls the immediate political effect of the group's statement among groups in the Boston left: "[W]e also drew many women of color or who were not Black to us. We had connections with Latinas. We had connections with Asian women. . . . And they drew us too. Because it wasn't just like one way. When we'd find out about things that were happening, we would get ourselves there as well."[21] The collective's principled stance on identity politics functioned as a principle of unity, rather than division.

But, in the decades since the founding of the Combahee River Collective, instead of forging alliances across difference, some have chosen to close ranks—especially on social media—around ever-narrower conceptions of group interests. Smith says, diplomatically, that many of today's common uses of the concept are "very different than what we intended."[22] Asad Haider puts it more starkly in his book *Mistaken Identity,* where he acknowledges the radical history of the concept while nevertheless describing identity politics as "the ideology that emerged to appropriate this emancipatory legacy in service of the advancement of political and economic elites."[23] While agreeing with these points, I also agree with political theorist Marie Moran and philosopher Linda Martín Alcoff who have both argued effectively that ideological explanations that tie troubling political developments to the ideas supposedly built into identity politics tend to miss the mark: many criticisms target ideas that aren't essential to identity-based movements or that misconstrue their basic goals entirely.[24]

The idea of "elite capture" helps reconcile these two points with each other. It is true that recent developments in the meaning and use of identity politics have not stopped police murders or emptied prisons. Identity politics has, however, equipped people, organizations, and institutions with a new vocabulary to describe their politics and aesthetic—even if the substance of those political decisions are irrelevant or even counter to the interests of the marginalized people whose identities are being deployed. But that is a feature of how identity politics is being used, rather than what identity politics is at its core. It is this "elite capture"—not identity politics itself—that stands between us and a transformative, nonsectarian, coalitional politics.

Elite Capture: The Bigger Problem

The concept of elite capture originated in the study of developing countries to describe the way socially advantaged people tend to gain control over financial benefits, especially foreign aid, meant for others. But the concept has also been applied more generally to describe how political projects can be hijacked in principle or in effect by the well positioned and resourced. And yet, the idea also helps to explain how public resources such as knowledge, attention, and values become distorted and distributed by power structures.

Elite capture accounts for many of the common objections leveled against identity politics, including that it requires uncritical support for political figures based on their identities without regard for their politics and that it often reflects social preoccupations that are "really for rich white people." One commentator, Saagar Enjeti, criticized "the identity politics obsessed elite wing of the Democratic party," alleging that "the people who populate our newsrooms" and "populate the professional managerial class . . . have far too much of an impact on our contemporary political discourse."[25] Despite having identified the problem with mainstream popular uses of identity politics today—the outsize impact of well-positioned people on our political discourse—Enjeti nevertheless seems to think this is a special problem of one wing of one political party. In fact, the underlying dynamics are as old as politics itself and are not confined to a particular politics of social identity.

Elite capture is not a conspiracy. It's bigger than cynical appropriations, opportunism, or the moral successes or failures of any individual or group. It is a kind of system behavior—a phenomenon articulated at the population level, an observable (predictable) pattern of actions involving individuals, groups, and subgroups, each of whom may be pursuing any number of different goals from their own narrow point of view. Elite capture is not limited to the scope of their intentions. The constant dynamic of individual and group interactions makes up a social system, and elite capture emerges out of that dynamic.

Systems and systems-level issues are big and complex, but they are not abstract. Social systems are real: after all, we live in them. As such, they are entities that we can observe and, frequently, anticipate. Our social sciences are, for better or worse, attempts to do exactly that. It is of course true that social systems are exceedingly complex—perhaps more so than physical systems, since they encompass them, plus quite a bit more besides. And, since our collective thinking about the system is itself an important part of the system we are analyzing, the very thing that we study shifts as we understand it differently, precisely *because* we understand it differently.

So if elite capture is bigger than the most nefarious plans of the biggest villains, is it also bigger than the best intentions of those who oppose them?

In reality, we may not be able to entirely eliminate elite capture from the world. Achieving radical equality in the distribution of resources and power is itself an idealized outcome of the social movements we support, rather than the sort of thing that could precede and produce their success. Much like rust emerges in different times and places where metal and water meet, elite capture emerges in different times and places where social systems encounter certain conditions (as I explain in chapter 3). But this book is motivated by the belief that when we can recognize elite capture happening, we have more options to combat it. This belief is paired with another central concern: recent trends in identity politics seem to be supercharging, rather than restraining, elite capture. As

I discuss in chapter 4, this is even true of the politics of deference: an etiquette that asks people to pass attention, resources,
and initiative to those perceived as more marginalized than
themselves.

We should respond to the problems of elite capture, and
the racial capitalism that enables it, not with deference politics
but with *constructive* politics. A constructive approach would
focus on outcome over process: the pursuit of specific goals or
results, rather than mere avoidance of "complicity" in injustice or promotion of purely moral or aesthetic principles. A
constructive approach fits squarely into what political theorist
Michael Dawson calls "pragmatic utopianism . . . that starts
where we are, but imagines where we want to be," combin-
ing a set of goals unbound by whatever passes for common
sense today with a "hardheaded political realism" capable of
finding the strategies and tactics needed to shift common
sense and the world underneath it.[26]

When it comes to knowledge and information, a constructive politics would be concerned primarily with building
institutions and campaign-relevant practices of information
gathering, rather than centering specific groups of people
or spokespeople who stand in for them. It would focus on
accountability, rather than conformity. It would calibrate itself directly to the task of redistributing social resources and
power, rather than to intermediary goals cashed out in pedestals or symbolism. It would focus on building and rebuilding rooms, not regulating traffic within and between them.
It would be what political scientist Adom Getachew terms
a "worldmaking" project, aimed at building and rebuilding

actual structures of social connection and movement, rather than mere critique of the ones we already have.[27]

This book is for the people who want to see different outcomes—those who want a different, and better, world system than the one we have now. It is not a how-to guide. Rather, it is intended to help people who are doing the hard work of changing the world to see certain trends and traps that beset organizing—and thus help them respond to their own particular contexts more strategically. To that end, I want to give the best explanation of my perspective on the underlying problem of elite capture—and the best explanation of constructive politics as a response to it—that I can. We can work out collectively where to go from there.

The remainder of this book aims to answer some key questions about why elite capture matters and what we should do about it. Chapter 1 elaborates a more in-depth answer to the question "What is elite capture?" Chapter 2 follows up on this description, using it to make some headway in identifying where elite capture shows up in our social conditions and why. With all this as background, by chapter 3 we will be in a position to understand why deference politics—a kind of culture that builds itself around identity politics—fuels the elite capture of identity politics. I wrap things up in chapter 4 with some thoughts about an alternative approach, which I call constructive politics.

1

What Is Elite Capture?

In 1957, E. Franklin Frazier published a controversial work of sociology: *Black Bourgeoisie*. This work was, among other things, a pioneering analysis of elite capture that will help clarify the basic phenomenon.

Edward Franklin Frazier was born to James and Mary Clark Frazier in Baltimore, Maryland, in 1894. Though his father had managed to teach himself to read and write without having ever attended school, those hard-won markers of respectability won him no exemptions from the degradations of working life as a Black man in a racist society. Nevertheless, James made it a point to impress upon his children the importance of education. Throughout his time in Baltimore public schools, Edward seemed to take it to heart, graduating near the top of his high school class. The reward for his hard work was a scholarship to Howard University.[1]

After graduating from Howard with honors, Frazier turned to teaching while continuing his studies. He was an instructor at the Tuskegee Institute in Alabama and eventually became director of social work at the Atlanta School of

Social Work. There, American sociology and Black sociology were both being invented by a network of Black scholars that included W. E. B. Du Bois. While their scholarship likely influenced his later thinking, Frazier's time there was limited, as he was fired in 1927—after which he and his wife, Marie, moved to Chicago, where Frazier completed a doctorate in sociology while teaching at Fisk University. In 1943, he was hired at Howard University in Washington, DC, where he stayed until his death.[2]

Frazier was uncommonly successful, especially for a Black academic of his era. That was certainly not because he played it safe. His views on the Black family launched historic debates with fellow sociologist Melville Herskovits, and they continue to shape scholarship and policy decades later.[3] His 1927 firing from Atlanta was set in motion when of one of his articles, "The Pathology of Race Prejudice," broke a taboo: it analyzed white Southerners with the same anthropological eye so often trained on "other" peoples. It probably didn't help smooth things over that Frazier argued white Southern racism toward Black people was a kind of insanity. His article was picked up by the *Atlantic Constitution*, a local paper, and soon the Fraziers were on the receiving end of death threats.[4] Good old "cancel culture" at work.

But the controversy for which Frazier is known best would not be kicked off until thirty years later, with the publication of his 1957 sociological study of the US Black middle class, *Black Bourgeoisie*. In the book, Frazier accuses the Black middle class of being an insecure, powerless group constantly constructing a world of "make-believe" to deal with an "inferiority complex" caused by the brutal history of racial domination in the United States. It was instantly controversial. Frazier recalls in a preface to the 1962 edition that in the aftermath of the first edition, he was both applauded for his courage and threatened with violence.

At around the same time as Frazier was analyzing the Black bourgeoisie of the United States, Frantz Fanon was publishing seminal works of political philosophy in which he discussed mid-century African middle classes. Their approaches bore striking similarities. Fanon was writing during the wave of national independence movements in Asia and Africa that followed the conclusion of the Second World War—a time of possibility and political questions. The African middle classes of which he spoke were poised to become the national ruling elite of post-colonial societies. He described this bourgeoisie as an "underdeveloped middle class" that was "not engaged in production, nor in invention, nor building, nor labor" and thus doomed to actions of the "intermediary type": that is, to "keep in the running and to be part of the racket."[5]

These failures of this new post-colonial ruling class explain, in part, why Fanon suspected that it would capture, dilute, and ultimately subvert the energy of anti-imperialist struggle.[6] "National consciousness," he predicted, "instead of being the all-embracing crystallization of the innermost hopes of the whole people, instead of being the immediate and most obvious result of the mobilization of the people, will be in any case only an empty shell, a crude and fragile travesty of what it might have been."[7]

This prediction seemed to come true. The national independence movements supplanted formal colonial rule only to run headfirst into neocolonialism: a condition in which those young nations' new ruling elite were either sharply constrained by or actively colluding with the corporations and governments of the former colonial powers—and the international system they dominated.[8] African studies scholar Georges Nzongola-Ntalaja, writing in the early 1980s, just after this wave of independence movements, summed it up this way:

> The masses had hoped that their living conditions would be improved after independence, and this was in fact what these leaders promised them. But the promise was not honored after independence, for many reasons, one of which was the fact that the anticolonial struggle had masked the conflicts of interested between the petty bourgeoisie and ordinary people. These conflicts became manifest after independence when, instead of fulfilling their promises, the new rulers responded to popular demands either with more promises or with repression.[9]

Why were the Black "lumpenbourgeoisie" (as Frazier described them) of the United States and the newly ascendant African ruling classes so ineffective at improving the systems for Black people as a group? Frazier and Fanon alike focused on their intellectual and political failures.

Fanon referred to a belief among the African middle classes that they could "advantageously replace the middle

class of the mother country," which he saw as "willful nar-
cissism" and "intellectual laziness."[10] Frazier was similarly un-
bridled in his criticisms, and some of the most scathing were
directed at the Black press, "the chief medium of communication which creates and perpetuates the world of make-believe for the black bourgeoisie." While acknowledging the
contributions of Black publications like the *Chicago Defender*
and early abolitionist organs like Frederick Douglass's *Paper*,
Frazier nevertheless insisted that the Black press's "demand for
equality for the Negro in American life is concerned primarily with opportunities which will benefit the black bourgeoisie economically and enhance the social status of the Negro."
The elite in control of prominent Black media, he argued,
would advance these subgroup interests seemingly without
regard to the welfare of the larger group. Frazier gave as an
example the celebration by Black newspapers of the election
of a Black doctor to the presidency of a local affiliate of the
American Medical Association, even though the doctor had
opposed a national health program and the AMA itself opposed "socialized medicine."[11] Good old respectability politics
at work.

A central argument of *Black Bourgeoisie* concerns a gen-
erations-old political strategy for racial uplift: the project of
building a separate Black economy within the United States.
Booker T. Washington's National Negro Business League,
which first convened in Boston, Massachusetts, in 1900, is a
classic example of this strategy, which debuted to great en-
thusiasm and fanfare among Black business leaders. Frazier,
however, argued that Washington's approach was misguided,

based on faulty analysis of the economic situation of African Americans at the time. The combined net worth of all 115 attendees at the inaugural National Negro Business League did not amount to even $1 million. By the time Frazier wrote his book, more than six decades later, all eleven Black-owned banks in the nation combined did not represent the amount of capital held in the average local bank in smaller white cities. Frazier thus concludes that an African American economy was a pipe dream all along.[12]

Not only would building a national Black economy be mathematically almost impossible, Frazier asserted; the attempt would also be politically naive. Such an economy would have to be bootstrapped out of the present political reality, which would make it vulnerable to outside influence—despite being a response to that very vulnerability. Even if people are successfully persuaded to "buy Black," Frazier argued, if they're doing so with dollars earned from their job at the Ford plant, then we haven't yet created a Black economy.

Why does the myth of a Black economy as a comprehensive response to anti-Black racism survive, even if prominent Black businesspeople have long been in a position to know that it wasn't a serious possibility? Frazier contends that it owes its persistence to the particular class interests of the small but influential Black bourgeoisie who were behind the idea. Some of these were business owners hoping to enjoy a monopoly of the African American economic market. Others were salaried professionals—far and away the largest percentage of the Black middle class in the mid-twentieth century—hoping to work their way into white-owned marketing firms on the strength of their presumed knowledge of the untapped potential of Black purchasing power in the Cold War economy.

Whether on the part of the Black press or the Black entrepreneurs, Frazier claims that "the black bourgeoisie have shown no interest in the 'liberation' of Negroes"—that is, unless "it affected their own status or acceptance by the white community."[13] Given half a chance, "the black bourgeoisie has exploited the Negro masses as ruthlessly as have whites."[14] Frazier surely overstates things here. Nonetheless, his book, like Fanon's work, offers a crisp depiction of elite capture that remains valuable.

Today, we are about as far in time from Frazier's *Black Bourgeoisie* and Fanon's *Black Skin, White Masks* as Frazier and Fanon were from Booker T. Washington's National Negro Business League. But little has changed. In his comprehensive analysis of the current state of this political trajectory, communication studies scholar Jared A. Ball reveals a set of political arrangements much like the one Frazier depicted more than a half century earlier. There have been some twists and turns: as Ball explains, the latest iteration of the mythical Black economy-to-freedom pipeline centers narrowly on African Americans' economic power as consumers rather than as bankers or as producers. According to the myth, Black Americans have over $1 trillion worth of power as consumers that they could use to bootstrap themselves into power and freedom, but instead squander on fashion and other frivolous purchases. This concept of "buying power," he argues, was developed by the US government and business elites and is maintained in implicit partnership with Black businesspeople and media elites—roughly the same cast of characters Frazier referred to as the Black "lumpenbourgeoisie."[15] Ball adds that the "buying power" variant of this myth also serves to shift focus and blame onto the supposed "financial illiteracy" of the Black poor, as opposed to the social and economic conditions that exploit, oppress, and marginalize people.[16]

Ball's analysis reiterates Frazier's: in each story, what lies behind the "movement for a Black economy" is a myth and a material reality. The possibility of an insulated Black economy is the myth, while the immediate interests of a few well-positioned Black folk provide the true impetus. And in both versions of the story, it is the problem—the institutions and patterns of the status quo—that is offered up as the solution.

Who Runs the World? Elites

Confronted with this problem that masquerades as solution, Frazier and Ball both get right something crucial that critics of "identity politics"—as well as "wokeness," "cancel culture," and many other hot-button terms—frequently get wrong. Critics and detractors of these political commitments claim that they reflect the social preoccupations of "rich white people" or the "professional-managerial class." And they're not completely wrong. But that fact is just something that identity politics, wokeness, and the like have in common with *everything else* in our lives: the increasing domination of elite interests and control over aspects of our social system. That's because almost everything in our social world has a tendency to fall prey to elite capture. In other words, it's not just that wokeness is too white. It's that *everything* is.

True, whiteness and eliteness are two very different things. For our purposes, though, this is a fair dig because they have gone hand in hand in many parts of the world for the past few hundred years, with consequences that have shaped everything around us.

The core concern of this book is eliteness as such—and there's no hard and fast rule about what kind of person can be an elite. Sometimes you're an elite because of how people have decided (or been forced) to relate to some aspect of your social identity. Sometimes you're an elite because of some more contingent advantage: your level of education, wealth, or social prestige. Sometimes you're an elite just because you happen to be the only one of your group who's in a particular room. According to political scientist Jo Freeman, "an elite refers to a small group of people who have power over a larger group of which they are part, usually without direct responsibility to that larger group, and often without their knowledge or consent."[17] You'll notice that Freeman doesn't treat the status of "elite" as a stable identity—it's a relationship, in a particular context, between a smaller group of people and a larger group of people.

Elite capture happens when the advantaged few steer resources and institutions that could serve the many toward their own narrower interests and aims. The term is used in economics, political science, and related disciplines to describe the way socially advantaged people tend to gain control over benefits meant for everyone.[18] In this context, it has been used much like the more familiar label of "corruption" and identified by similar symptoms of undue influence, such as bribes.[19] But the concept has also been applied to describe how political projects more generally can be hijacked—in principle or in effect—by the well positioned and better resourced.

As economist Diya Dutta explains, elite capture, in essence, refers to "the presence of unequal access to power—some have greater access to power (by virtue of their lineage, or caste, or economic wealth or gender or some other reason) and consequently the ability to influence the transfer of funds/resources disproportionately."[20] Public goods and resources such as knowledge, attention, and values are unfairly distributed, just as much as material wealth and political power are. More precisely, the distribution patterns of all these are distorted in similar ways, for similar reasons. Elite capture is symptomatic of social systems with unequal balances of power.

Does Democracy Matter?

If liberal political theory offered an accurate view of the world (which it doesn't), then one might conclude that the balance of power in many areas of the world is already okay. Many places in the world are self-proclaimed democracies, after all, and the democratic system is supposed to be all about a healthy balance of power. In democracies, ostensibly, the elites (policymakers) are put in office by the non-elites (citizens), who can remove and replace them if they fail to defend public interests. Much like the mythical market, mythical liberal democracy is supposed to be self-correcting and self-justifying by definition. This way of casting the conversation about power and governance has been integral to the framing that links "freedom" and "capitalism" in the ideals and practices of liberal democracy: a country's freedom need only be found at its ballot boxes rather than in, say, its workplaces.[21] Thus, if one believes in liberal democracy, they may believe that imbalances of power everywhere could be fixed by instituting arrangements like the "rules-based international order," "democratic elections," and "formal political representation." In a nutshell, if the right ideals are embodied in the right formal systems, then the outcomes of those systems are justified.

To be clear, formal arrangements *do* matter. Phrases like "formal political representation" are genuinely meaningful, given that places with less formal political representation *do* tend to operate differently than places with more. But these phrases get bandied about in ways that are often less than meaningful. So if we want to hang our hopes on the ideals of democratic accountability, we should take stock of how far we are from actually achieving even this low bar for control over our own lives. After decades of this liberal democratic rhetoric, actual decision-making structures rarely rely on actual democratic accountability.

We are likeliest to talk about elite capture at the national level. In her book *From #BlackLivesMatter to Black Liberation*, Princeton professor Keeanga-Yamahtta Taylor cites the telling example of the Congressional Black Caucus's cosponsorship of

Ronald Reagan's 1986 Anti–Drug Abuse Act, which helped supercharge mass incarceration by establishing mandatory minimum sentencing guidelines and adding $1.7 billion toward the drug war, while welfare programs were cut.[22] This legislation solved a problem for the Reaganites and the Black elites of the Congressional Black Caucus alike, allowing them to look busy with respect to the crack cocaine epidemic. But with the law's passage, working-class African Americans went from dealing with one very complex problem to weathering two interlocking ones: the drug epidemic itself—unsolved by this draconian measure—and the surge of discriminatory law enforcement the legislation unleashed. These consequences led Democratic senator Daniel Patrick Moynihan to make a striking appraisal: "If we blame crime on crack, our politicians are off the hook. Forgotten are failed schools, the malign welfare programs, the desolate neighborhoods, the wasted years. Only crack is to blame. One is tempted to think that if crack did not exist, someone somewhere would have received a federal grant to develop it."[23]

It is often alleged that the federal government was directly responsible for the crack epidemic.[24] However, not much hinges on whether there was an active conspiracy. For a combination of laziness, callous indifference, and opportunism was perfectly sufficient: the elites at the levers of funding and oversight saw what was in their own best interest and then simply did that; its foreseeable negative effects on those they supposedly represent weren't an effective deterrent.

And then there's capital. The 1950s and 60s saw important innovations in corporate management (particularly in the

United States, which stood comfortably atop the post-World War II global economy): leveraged buyouts, divestitures, mergers, major sell-offs of "non-core-businesses," and other forms of reorganization of businesses by profit-hungry share-holders.[25] These trends intensified in the 1980s, producing what researchers call the "shareholder revolution": a prolifer-ation of management techniques that put previously compla-cent industry managers under the strict discipline of activist shareholders.[26] This second phase of shareholder revolution coincided with and helped produce a larger "global business revolution," a "fast-developing process of concentration at a global level in numerous industries supplying goods and ser-vices" to "systems integrators"—the few large firms who can reorganize global production around their "core" business model and assets.[27]

The elites atop "system integrator" mega-corporations have not stopped at reorganizing global production around their pursuit of shareholder value. In fact, they are reorganiz-ing everything. Corporations have built their own shadow court system of "arbitration," effectively removing entire industries from even the barest pretense of judicial review.[28] Public service projects across the world, but especially in the global South, have been financed by "public-private partner-ships": "long-term contractual arrangements through which the private sector commits to finance and manage public ser-vices . . . as long as the state shares the risks." Economists Ndongo Samba Sylla and Daniela Gabor explain that this has functioned in ways characteristic of racial capitalism: build-ing financial security for shareholders by way of financial and other forms of precarity for the people in countries like Senegal and the Ivory Coast who are charged high user fees to access privately financed infrastructure.[29] Making matters worse, social media tech giants own huge swaths of the world's attention economy, running platforms that are rife with abuse—a 2021 investigation by journalist Karen Hao found that the largest Facebook pages targeting "Christian Americans" and "African Americans" were run by troll farms exploiting Facebook algorithms to send information to tens of millions of Americans with the aim of inflaming and exploiting social divisions. These farms also operate in India, the United Kingdom, and throughout Central and South America.[30]

But elite capture is perhaps clearest at the multinational level, where weighty decisions about economic possibilities are made by large global institutions without even the pretense of democratic accountability. These institutions emerged as the world order was being reconstructed in the waning years of the Second World War, with the United States newly emergent as a global hegemon. The architects met in Bretton Woods, New Hampshire, where they set up the International Monetary Fund (IMF) and what later became the World Bank. Whatever the narrow "technical" pretensions of their mandates, these organizations in fact have immense governing power. They offer aid packages that are conditional on certain governance decisions by the receiving country—decisions that help determine the availability of jobs, public services, and the price of food. These basic features of non-elite life are thus placed in the hands of foreign bureaucrats over whom the country's population have no means of democratic control, nor even the pretense of any sort of democratic relationship.[31]

The 1980s featured a particularly controversial set of "structural adjustment programs" through which the IMF strong-armed governments into liberalizing markets and devaluing currency in order to qualify for needed loans.[32] And why did they need the loans badly enough to take such a deal? Broadly, because colonial governments had expropriated so much value from the colonies, in a myriad of ways, for centuries. The World Bank and IMF continue to encourage post-colonial nations to maintain high levels of predatorily securitized debt today. By maintaining financial control, they operate as de facto governing bodies, tying needed aid to politically distorting conditions.[33]

The control exerted by these Bretton Woods institutions lacks even the aesthetic of democracy. Since voting power is allocated by measures of wealth rather than population, middle- and low-income countries (much of the global South) have a minority share of votes despite making up 85 percent of the world's population.[34] The process of voting in these institutions is thus skewed in the direction of yesterday's power blocs, rather than today's needs. Moreover, the heads of the World Bank and IMF are typically from the United States and Europe and are nominated by these states, not elected in any sense (even a skewed one).

There have been genuine attempts to defy the World Bank and IMF. For decades, Latin Americans have elected populist leaders in response to the most recent developments in neoliberal capitalism. But the results have been mixed, and the failures have been bloody. Ecuador, for example, has experienced decades of conflict between "radical resource nationalists" and "anti-extractivists," a debate that was made possible (if not inevitable) by the country's dependence on fossil fuel extraction for the revenue that funds its social projects and services its sovereign debt.[35]

Over the decades between the Second World War and the present, the functional partnership between capitalism and liberal democracy, with its semblance of popular legitimacy, has weakened across the globe. It is for this reason that legal scholar Issa Shivji describes liberal democracy as being "under siege." In his view, it is in decline because of the sociological traps set by monopoly capitalism: "jobless growth, inequitable distribution, and unbearable inequality," and the resulting alienation of much of the population from the political system.[36] Similarly, sociologist Wolfgang Streeck argues that the liberal democratic ideal has been disintegrating for decades. Rather than a cataclysmic putsch or violent event, for Streeck, the end of democracy simply *is* the gradual capture of the political by the elites: "[A]s one crisis followed the next, and the fiscal crisis of the state unfolded alongside them, the arena of distributional conflict shifted, moving upwards and away from the world of collective action of citizens towards ever more remote decision sites where interests appear as 'problems' in the abstract jargon of technocratic specialists."[37]

Capture at Every Scale

Streeck describes some common features of elite capture: less collective action by people, more remote decision sites, and the rise of technocrats. Such shifts are visible not only at the level of national and international policy, but at smaller levels of organization as well.

Take, for example, the section of the world where I work: the ivory tower. In *Philosophy of African American Studies*, North Carolina State University professor Stephen Ferguson II describes the elite capture of Black studies, which owes its existence to the radical student movements of the 1960s and '70s but has since been "turned into a bureaucratic cog in the academic wheel controlled by administrators, with virtually no democratic input from students or the Black working-class community."[38]

This is not a special feature of the ivory tower's influence on Black politics. The Combahee River Collective formed in part because of failures of solidarity across several overlapping axes of difference: gender lines within Black liberation struggles, racial lines within women's liberation movements, and sexuality lines within Black feminist organizations. Neither these tensions nor the forms of elite capture they represent were new in their day: Angela Davis's *Women, Race, and Class* presents a masterful analysis of similar forms of capture by the best positioned feminists during the anti-slavery and early women's rights movements of the nineteenth century.[39] Some scholars argue that E. Franklin Frazier himself exemplified some of these tendencies, tying social problems in the

Black community too closely with the prevalence of women-headed households.[40]

Or, instead of broadening the context we look for elite capture within, we could maintain the same scale but reverse the identities. That is: instead of thinking about the class politics of racial studies, one could describe the race politics of class activism, where we might find that whites (racial elites) tend to capture the decision-making process of socialist organizations, labor unions, and the like.[41]

Elite capture is not particular to Black politics. Take, for example, the last few decades of queer politics, illustrated in the aptly titled essay "You Wanted Same-Sex Marriage? Now You Have Pete Buttigieg." *BuzzFeed* writer Shannon Keating laments the gradual trajectory of mainstream queer politics away from the more radical and progressive elements dramatized by the 1969 Stonewall riots and the confrontational organizing of New York's AIDS Coalition to Unleash Power (ACT UP), toward assimilationist goals of being represented by, and treated like, Democratic politicians such as Buttigieg—telegenic, monogamous, white, financially secure, and vocally Christian. As Keating says, "The best way for queer people to get ahead, it seems, is still to act as though we are *just like everybody else*."[42] Barbara Smith, one of the original organizers of the Combahee River Collective (who, as described in chapter 1, came up with the term "identity politics"), left active involvement in the mainstream LGBTQ movement for this reason.[43]

When we look at uneven distributions of power, at every scale, in every context, the patterns of elite capture eventually show up. In the absence of the right kind of checks or constraints, the subgroup of people with power over and access to the resources used to describe, define, and create political realities—in other words, the elites—will capture the group's values, forcing people to coordinate on a narrower social project that disproportionately represents elite interests. When elites run the show, the interests of the group get whittled down to what they have in common with those at the top, at best. At worst, elites fight for their own narrow interests using the banner of group solidarity.

This chapter has tried to make good on something I claim in the introduction: that elite capture is a general political problem, not a special one faced by antiracist or identity politics alone. Noticing *that* elite capture shows up across our global social system is a good start. But if we are going to do something about it, it would also help to know *why*.

2

Reading the Room

Anne Eliza Riddle was in an uncommon position. Maybe her mistress was just unusually enthusiastic about reading. Or perhaps it had something to do with the fact that Anna was unusually fair skinned—rumor had it that one of her grandfathers was white. In which case Anna's mistress might well have also been Anna's aunt. Either way, her mistress broke the law, and so Anna was put in the uncommon position of being an enslaved Black person who knew how to read.

Whatever the merits of this small kindness by the planter family, it was overshadowed by the harsh realities of racial slavery, including the fact that they responded to financial difficulties in Anna's adolescence by threatening to sell her mother and two youngest brothers. Heroically, the teenaged Anna offered herself on the auction block to keep the rest of her family together. But she didn't fetch high-enough bids, so the planter family reverted to the original plan, tragically breaking up their family.[1]

A few years later, during the US Civil War, James Henry Woodson also found himself in an uncommon position in

Confederate territory. James was on the run. His owner had loaned him and his labor to a man who put him to work digging ditches, but James had used his spare time to make traps and furniture to sell and make money for himself. One day, the man found James working on precisely this. Furious at this affront, he tried to whip James—but James, knowing that the Union Army was nearby, hit him back and fled to his owner's house. He explained the situation as a "falling out," which to his aggravated owner sounded like a symptom of a much bigger problem. "Fell out! That's the trouble now! All free! All free," the white man exclaimed. And James replied, "Yes, we are free. . . . And if you bother me, I'll kill you, another devil." And off he went again.[2]

But James did not simply run *away* from the white planter he had threatened; he turned east, toward Richmond, Virginia, where he'd heard he could find Union soldiers. James did indeed meet some soldiers, and he told them his story. He led them first to the man who had so recently tried to whip him, and the soldiers "punished" the planter. Then James took them to various Confederate supply stations and warehouses, helping the Union to ransack the Southern army's supplies. He spent the rest of the Civil War scouting for the Union Army in much the same way. In so doing, James joined the ranks of the many enslaved African Americans who engaged in sabotage, withdrew their labor, and fought militarily—the "general strike," in the words of W. E. B. Du Bois, that helped defeat the Confederacy and destroy the system of racial slavery.[3]

Anna and James married shortly after the war, in 1867. The iron-willed couple tried their hand at the deeply rigged game of sharecropping, managing to scrape together enough money to buy a small farm in West Virginia. There, in 1875, they had their fourth child: Carter Godwin Woodson. Farm life was hard work, requiring the efforts of the entire family, but Anna made sure Carter and his siblings also received an education. They spent four months of the year in a one-room schoolhouse run by two of Anna's brothers who had also learned to read. This meant that Carter was both the child and student of former slaves.[4]

When Carter was seventeen, he found a job working in the coal mines of West Virginia. When one of his coworkers, a Black Civil War veteran, found out that Carter could read, the Black miners hatched a plan: they would pool their money to subscribe to the African American run *Richmond Planet* as well as several white daily newspapers, and Carter would read the papers aloud to the group. These reading and discussion groups helped Carter learn more and more about the wider world.

But he didn't stop there. Carter breezed through four years' worth of high school courses in two and took college courses at Berea, a rare racially integrated college in Kentucky founded by the abolitionist John Fee in 1855—all while serving, first, as an instructor at a school for miners' children, then, as principal of a school for African Americans.[5] After winning the Spanish–American War of 1898, the United States took over colonial possession of the Philippines from the Spanish—affording Carter, a US citizen, the opportunity to make a decent salary in the new colony teaching English and farming by day, while learning Spanish, French, and European history by night.

Using this knowledge and savings, Carter traveled throughout Asia, Africa, and Europe, learning about their education systems and attending lectures on the history of different places as he went. He returned to the United States in 1907 determined to become a scholar and correct history's silence about Black people: both the racist exclusion of African Americans from US history and widespread ignorance of and disinterest in African history.[6] After picking up a second undergraduate degree and a master's degree at the University of Chicago, he enrolled at Harvard University, where he earned a PhD in history. He was only the second African American to do so, after W. E. B. Du Bois.[7]

Despite having a PhD, Woodson was not destined for a steady life in academia. He was uncompromising in his standards, which put him at odds with many of the people who may have otherwise helped his academic career. In 1919, freshly arrived at Howard University, he created the university's first African American history course; the very next year, he came under the scrutiny of the administration for criticizing his employer in a major newspaper. This was the height of the Red Scare—the Russian Revolution of 1917 had just panicked elites the world over—and Senator Reed Smoot had criticized the university for having in its library a pamphlet on "the Bolsheviks and the Soviets."[8] When Howard's president ordered the item pulled from the collection, Carter couldn't keep quiet, and he soon found himself without a job.

But employed as such or not, Carter G. Woodson remained a scholar. He had already founded the *Journal of Negro History*, through which he continued his pioneering work in African American history by producing scholarship to his own exacting standard, and supporting young and emerging scholars, including Zora Neale Hurston. He also founded the Association for the Study of Negro Life and History (today known as the Association for the Study of African American Life and History), supported by a grassroots fundraising effort. Through Negro history clubs in high schools, theatrical renditions of historical events, and posters, the organization spread knowledge of Black history across the country.[9] His books were among those secretly used by Black educators nationwide to subvert white control over what Black schoolchildren learned. All of these efforts contributed to the broader network of intellectually insurgent practices of Black scholars and educators that education scholar Jarvis Givens calls "fugitive pedagogy."[10]

According to Howard University historian Daryl Michael Scott, Woodson believed that publishing "scientific history" would transform race relations. Scott points out that during the civil rights movement a few years later, Carter's approach to history was taught in the Freedom Schools that organizers set up across the South. "The Negro History movement," he explains, "was an intellectual insurgency that was part of every larger effort to transform race relations."[11]

But why did Carter think that an intellectual movement could seriously challenge a political structure?

Carter G. Woodson was a historian, and he was arguably a philosopher as well. This is apparent in much of his work, but especially in the 1933 book *The Mis-Education of the Negro*, in which he explains how elite capture structures societies' education systems. Woodson's keen insights provide a blueprint for a more general process that occurs at many levels and in many contexts throughout our social lives.

In the previous chapter, I noted the astonishing extent of elite capture: how many of our institutions, resources, and even political agendas evidence the direct control or significantly disproportionate influence of the most advantaged among us. But I haven't yet described, in a rich and textured sense, what elite capture *is*, at bottom. Understanding this might help explain why elite capture shows up in so many different parts of human social life, from the education system to the housing market; from the small-scale internal dynamics of an activist group to the massive scale of a government. But more importantly, understanding what elite capture is could help us identify it when we see it—and having identified it, to at least plot strategies to curb its worst excesses in our movements and in our own lives.

A trip through a fairy tale, accompanied by some philosophers and game theorists, will help us clarify what elite capture is—and why we see it everywhere we turn.

The Ground We Stand On

You've no doubt heard the story of the emperor who had no clothes. As Hans Christian Andersen told it, functionaries of the emperor handed him a hanger, claiming that it held a garment made of a mystical fabric that would appear invisible to anyone incompetent or exceptionally stupid. In fact, the hanger held nothing at all. The emperor put on the "garment" and walked around the town naked. Having heard of the myth claiming that, to point out the obvious, nakedness would confirm one's own incompetence and unintelligence, none of his subjects dared to point out the obvious—not even the servant assigned to hold the "train" of his nonexistent garment. The spell holds even as the emperor is escorted through the town in a celebratory parade. Finally, a young child yells: "But he hasn't got anything on." The spell is broken.

Like most fables, this story encapsulates deep insights about the social world. One insight is about how our interactions with each other are fundamentally structured by power. It's tempting to explain our oppressive social hierarchies and structures in terms of our sincere commitments: our beliefs, attitudes, and tightly held ideologies. When we look at things this way, we see racism as a way of thinking about one's place in the world (as "supreme," as "human") and a set of beliefs about others' place, misogyny as a way of looking at the masculine and the feminine (aggrandizing the former, disrespecting the latter), and so on.

This way of understanding phenomena in terms of ideology or belief has merit: surely what we genuinely believe about ourselves, what this world is like, and what we owe to each other all *affects* how we move through the world. But the relationship between what each of us takes to be true and good, and how we manage our specific day-to-day interactions is a lot more tenuous than this approach suggests, which is one of the insights that the story of the naked emperor seems tailor-made to share with us.

The interaction between the emperor and the crowd is one illustration of how as we talk or interact, we build the world together. Words, gestures, and signs don't interpret themselves; it's up to their users and observers to make something out of them. Communication is a kind of "joint action" in which each individual is playing their part in a thing *we're* doing together.[12] Accordingly, philosophers of language have often emphasized that we have to share to communicate. Among these things we share is information: after all, if we had to start from scratch, constructing our basic picture of the world every time we started a conversation, it would be hard to ever talk about anything interesting or do anything remotely complicated together. Instead, when we communicate, we presume certain "common beliefs" or "mutual beliefs"—not just things that *I* know and that *you* know, but things I-know-that-you-know, you-know-that-I-know, and so on.[13]

Philosopher Robert Stalnaker calls this public information the "common ground," likening it to a shared resource that participants in a conversation use to build and perform social interactions.[14] As we move through the world, the "ground" shifts beneath us. We add things to the common ground when we share information and perspectives. Our collective responses to events happening around us create new common ground over time. And we change the common ground when we use our words to challenge and reshape it, from defying personal rumors to renewing long-held cultural wisdom. Each of these interactions changes what information we treat as public and shared.

What's important about this public information is what we do with it. When we act in social contexts, we treat the information in the common ground *as if it were true*: that is, we treat it as a premise for public action.[15] Use of this common bank of assumptions is ubiquitous in social life: its because we share so many assumptions about meals and socializing that my partner telling me that friends are coming over tonight suffices to get me to cook more food and set extra places at the dinner table. Similarly, the townsfolk in the fable treat a naked emperor, presumed clothed, as the premise of their shared activity of cheering. And this makes sense of their choice to cheer, at one level. But, as the fable's setting dramatizes, there are all kinds of reasons to act as if something is true.[16] Genuine belief is just one potential reason among many.

The rise of social media has made us hyperaware of something that has always been true about communication: the social world in which we talk to each other is complex, and what we want out of interactions often goes far beyond what we're saying on the surface. We aim to manage relationships and reputations; to pursue clout or to frustrate someone else's attempt to do the same; to bolster our "side" of disputes that are political (in senses both grand and small); to gain resources and rewards or to avoid punishments and obstacles.

Much like common sense, common ground isn't always quite as "common" as advertised. On a good day, we communicate in good faith and for good reasons. Maybe we accept a new idea that challenges our previous perspective and incorporate it into our sense of the common. We do that as part of meaningfully sharing the world with the people around us, trusting that they too communicate in good faith and for good reasons.

We may accept new information into the common ground because we believe this information to be true, and reject old information because we believe it to be false—certainly this is the way the scientists of the world would like things to proceed—and we care about tending to the quality of our common ground to the extent that our ability to live and flourish together depends on it. This, at least, is a picture of the way that the common ground might work in a social context in which we distribute trust, respect, and authority in just and fair ways, and where we communicate in ways that seek the common good. Sounds nice, doesn't it?

Our social contexts are, of course, much less rosy than that.

Consider a different scenario. This one comes from the philosopher of language David Lewis.[17] Lewis, true to the detached style of so-called analytic philosophers, introduces the example as a dry, bloodless thought experiment: "For some reason—coercion, deference, common purpose—two people are both willing that one of them should be under the control of the other. (At least within certain limits, in a certain sphere of action, so long as certain conditions prevail.) Call one the *slave*, the other the *master*. The control is exercised verbally, as follows."[18] But this framing is deceptive. Since slavery was an actual social institution, Lewis is in effect describing rules of communication that governed actual interactions that were part and parcel of the construction of racial capitalism and the global political system it produced.

Still, let's stay with this bloodless thought experiment for just a moment. A master speaking to their slave occupies a position of power that decides what is communicatively possible when they interact. For example, their refusal to consider the possibility that it is raining outside rules out ways of speaking that presume that it is raining. It is in the nature of their social relationship—and, as a result, of their conversations—that this power relationship only goes one way. The slave's experience of the rain, however direct, is not eligible to contribute to shared understandings. The common ground is not a democratically governed resource, for the same reason none of the other resources around them are: they live in a slave society.

Communication is often described in overly intellectual terms that take its role as information exchange a bit too seriously. On such views, to have one's offer of public information unfairly rejected is to be harmed in some special "epistemic" way "as a knower."[19] The systems of injustice that show up in our communicative interactions are then frequently treated as a special ideological kind of injustice, rooted in a belief system that stands apart from or even behind other systems of injustice.[20]

But another possibility is that communication is simply a kind of action, and thus that the way we act in conversation is largely governed by the exact same forces, norms, and incentives that explain everything else we do. Elites "capture" our conversations, then, for largely the same reasons and in the same ways as they capture everything else.

What are the townspeople who cheer the naked emperor thinking? We could, if we wanted to, build an intricate intellectual architecture to explain why the townspeople cheer. We could imagine that they are true believers, with a whole complex of legitimizing myths. Maybe both the emperor and the townspeople are genuinely persuaded by the false story of the invisible garment because they believe *another* false story about the emperor's unique insight into the deep structure of reality, or because they believe in some supernatural mechanism that punishes personal faults with hallucinations. This is the kind of explanation that people often give when they try to explain oppression by appeal to "implicit bias," "ideology," "epistemic injustice," or cultural explanations rooted in the moral and spiritual rot of oppressive societies.

Something is wrong with *the townspeople themselves*, these explanations seem to say. So, if we want to know why the townspeople are behaving this strange way on this strange day, we had better figure out what ails them psychologically or culturally, or in some other dimension that shapes their perceptions and intuitions. Surely those who adopt this perspective are onto *something*. It would be hard to imagine that a society could demand slavish conversational obedience across days, years, and generations without any ramifications whatsoever on how people actually think and feel about the world, and act in it.

But we get a different answer if we ask not why the townspeople *believe* the emperor, but rather why they are acting *as if* they believe the emperor. Put another way, from this perspective it is not *beliefs* that are being systematically organized, but *behavior*. This way of thinking about the situation still allows the possibility that the townspeople in fact hold belief structures that inform their behavior. But unlike the first approach, it concerns itself seriously with what's in it for the townsfolk if they play along—and what's at stake for them if they do not.

If people make communicative decisions for the same kinds of reasons that they take other actions, then the whole situation becomes much less mysterious. The question of what all those townspeople cheering the naked emperor were thinking might simply and plausibly be: "If I don't play along with the emperor, something bad might happen to me."

This adjustment might seem slight, but it clarifies one reason to be dissatisfied with the kinds of explanations that involve beliefs and attitudes and culture: in taking the formal justifications for hierarchical interactions a little too seriously, they risk deeply misunderstanding what's really happening between people, especially when it comes to abusive interactions. Robin D. G. Kelley and James C. Scott have convincingly argued that even their fellow professional historians are prone to this sort of error, in their tendency to mistake broad swaths of history during which oppressed populations have "played along" with oppressive systems for evidence that they were "true believers" in those systems.[21] Indeed, some of them were as far from true believers as you can imagine: tricksters playing along with a social script even while they craftily resisted the powers that be.[22]

We don't have to assume that the baker and candlestick maker, who the naked emperor passes on the street as they are just trying to get through their days, have any interest at all in the question of whether or not the emperor is, in fact, clothed. We could guess that their guiding interests are in selling that day's bread and candles—that is, in keeping food on the table and tax collectors off their back. Standing behind their immediate state of mind as they watch the emperor come into view will be personal histories and pieces of common ground. Perhaps both citizens know the fairy tale of the commoner who becomes a nobleman because the emperor is so delighted with his wares. Or they might have in the back of their minds the much more probable, even mundane story of a businessman imprisoned or publicly tortured for unpaid debts or insulting the imperial throne.

There are many possible backstories that could lead a baker and a candlestick maker to set up shop on a street the emperor sometimes parades down, and that could shape their thoughts as they see him approach, and not one of them is about what the emperor is or isn't wearing—nor about what the baker or candlestick maker really believes about what the emperor is wearing. Yet it turns out that these kinds of stories do an adequate job all on their own of explaining why a baker and candlestick maker might play along with whatever an emperor expects them to do that day.

All it takes to understand this story is to stare patiently at what authority *is* and how it functions to organize social life.

The problem, it turns out, isn't the emperor's townspeople at all, or even the emperor. It's the *town*. It's the empire.

The Theory of Miseducation

Enough with the metaphors. The point is clear enough, when simply stated: our political structures affect the structure of all of our interactions.[23] This is the point that Carter G. Woodson's travels throughout the world made to him very powerfully, and because his analysis remains so potent, we're going to dive into it a little further.

One of Woodson's critiques is more or less about Black political strategy. The "so-called modern education" being provided to Black students, Woodson felt, was rather like the "special systems set up by private agencies and governments to educate the natives in their colonies and dependencies" and "worked out in conformity to the needs of those who have enslaved and oppressed weaker peoples."[24] It was meant to confer diplomas and other markers of social prestige and distinction to select groups of African Americans, for whom removal from the rest of the Black community was generally both the reward and the cost. As a program of "racial uplift," he said, this amounted to an attempt to transform Black people *themselves* in the image of an oppressive society. A better mission would be to change the social conditions of their oppression.

His second critique, concerning the content of the education available to Blacks, further connects the dots. Woodson pointed out that the curricula being taught were all built around information selected as important by the dominant racist education system. He provides a memorable example in the third chapter of *Mis-Education*:

> In medical schools Negroes were likewise convinced of their inferiority in being reminded of their role as germ carriers. The prevalence of syphilis and tuberculosis among Negroes was especially emphasized without showing that these maladies are more deadly among the Negroes for the reason that they are Caucasian dis-

eases; and since these plagues are new to Negroes, these sufferers have not had time to develop against them the immunity which time has permitted in the Caucasian. Other diseases to which Negroes easily fall prey were mentioned to point out the race as an undesirable element when this condition was due to the Negroes' economic and social status. Little emphasis was placed upon the immunity of the Negro from diseases like yellow fever and influenza which are so disastrous to whites. Yet, the whites were not considered inferior because of this differential resistance to these plagues.[25]

Woodson's description refers to teachers' reports of medical information about African American populations. He doesn't dispute the numbers—the teachers were adding *accurate* information into the common ground. Nevertheless, Woodson contends, this information served to support racism. That's because of what was in the common ground already: a picture of the world in which statistical information about diseases prevalent among Black people fit naturally into prevailing and preexisting narratives about their uncleanliness and inferiority, whereas equivalent information about diseases disproportionately prevalent among whites fit into preexisting narratives around their superiority. The racism was not necessarily embedded in this particular sentence, this particular instance of communication, but in the narrative in which it was embedded.

Woodson paints a vivid picture of how the background system of power structures classroom interactions in ways that are complex—but also, if we're being real, well understood.

It's exactly the same dynamics that assure the naked emperor he can count on fawning compliments about his robe. There is no balanced reporting, no symmetrical communication possible in an imperial classroom. That asymmetry in education was a product, and Woodson knew it—he had studied in the halls where it was produced.

Carter G. Woodson's first understanding of how power shapes history came early. As a young coal miner in West Virginia, he had spent years learning about the Civil War from people who had actually fought in it. This education included animated debates between coworkers at the railroad yard where his father, James, worked alongside many former Confederates—debates that their employer put an end to after an argument between James and his ex-Confederate foreman came to blows.

Later, as a graduate student at Harvard University, Woodson studied under towering historians like Edward Channing, who would go on to win the Pulitzer Prize. Channing argued in his seminar not only that African Americans had no distinctive history, but also that they had had no important role in major historical events, including the US Civil War. Woodson pushed back against his professor, who challenged him to prove his point of view. Little did Channing know, his student's intention to do just that was a major reason he was studying at Harvard in the first place. Indeed, Carter was already well aware that the textbooks citing men like Channing coddled and elevated the perspectives that empowered people like James Woodson's foreman, and ignored the perspective of those like James.

These experiences inspired Woodson to produce a different kind of history: African American history. Through the *Journal of Negro History*, and the educational institutions he founded, he went on to produce a Black history that met his own exacting academic standards.

The point was not just to change hearts and minds, but to change the *common ground*—to change what information was *usable* by people in their daily interactions.

Elite Capture: Game It Out

In *Mis-Education*, Carter shares a number of valuable insights into the nature of communication, politics, history, and education, and this book will not do justice to all of them. Most pressing, for our purposes, are his insights into the political philosophy of language, as they help us get very close to understanding elite capture. And they yield even more insight when placed in conversation with another area of philosophy that also thinks about our interactions with each other in structured environments: namely, the philosophy of games.

In *Games: Agency as Art*, philosopher C. Thi Nguyen explains the key differences between *game worlds* and *real worlds*, and what we can learn about the second from the first.[26] Games have lower stakes: if my character "dies," if I fall behind in the Mario Kart race, we can just turn the console off and start over. They also feature an artificially clear decision-making environment: I know exactly what my goals should be and how to relate to others. Say, for example, that we're playing basketball. If they are wearing the same jersey that I'm wearing, then I help them score points, or score them myself; if they're wearing the other jersey, I try to stop them. The low stakes of games allow us to immerse ourselves in a world of make-believe where everything we do has a clear and instrumental relationship to our success.

This clear and instrumental relationship is one of the important ways that games fail to capture the complications and precarities of daily life—and doubtless part of why they make such great escapes. Our interactions with our young children, adult siblings, and aging parents are often fraught with complicated practical, psychic, and moral risks. Looming behind our everyday interactions with bosses and coworkers is the threat of failure, even joblessness (especially frightening in the United States, where joblessness carries the additional risks of houselessness and lack of health care). These high stakes would be easier to manage, perhaps, if it were just a little clearer how to play them—if there were one definitive parenting book, if you could "Neutralize Your Abusive Boss with One Weird Trick." Instead, we have to balance our own goals and needs with guesses we make about others' goals and needs, often hastily, and generally with little feedback along the way about how well we've done—except when the consequences of our mistakes speak for themselves.

The artificial clarity of game worlds is an important part of what makes them fun. Game designers build environments that give players clearer reasons to take specific actions, and the satisfaction of knowing that each action contributes to success or failure. While the clarity and simplicity of games distinguish them from our non-game experiences, that feeling that every move you make is crucial to your overall strategy of survival isn't entirely different from what occurs in actual life. As we saw in the case of the baker and the candlestick maker, power structures, like fictional environments, give people reasons to *play along*.

The potential overlap between this feature of many games and features of actual social environments is at the core of a real-world process that Nguyen describes as "value capture." Value capture is a process by which we begin with rich and subtle values, encounter simplified versions of them in the social wild, and revise our values in the direction of simplicity—thus rendering them inadequate. This kind of process is always a possible result of social interaction, but the distortions to our values are sharpest in social systems and environments where this simplicity is built into the structures of reward and punishment.

Capitalism itself is such a system: it rewards the relentless and single-minded pursuit of profit and growth—extremely narrow value systems that exclude much of what makes life worth living. But societies organized around fundamentalisms (whether religious or secular) and war have resulted in similarly warped value systems long before capitalism arrived on the scene.

In real life, the value capture process is sometimes deliberately managed by elites to manipulate and control others with game design–like tactics. Gig economy platforms like Uber and Lyft use "badges" and rating systems to manage the decision-making environment of their driver employees.[27] Even outside of work, social media features such as likes, shares, and retweets play the role of points in games. Over time, these simple metrics threaten to distort or take the place of values (say, the wish to meaningfully contribute to discussion or to take pride in the quality of one's work) that might otherwise have inflected our behavior on these platforms.

What unites these different stories is the nature of the value capture process itself. The employee who wants to do a good job may start out with complex motivations—for example, working hard while staying safe and conserving enough of their physical and emotional energy for themselves and their loved ones. Under pressure from the game-inspired environment created by her boss, however, the worker must focus on winning the tokens that communicate success to that boss, ultimately replacing the worker's initial value structure at the cost of the things it protected. For example, Disney and Amazon use obsessive "real-time worker productivity tracking" to induce employees to compete in a ratings system based on speed or volume of production.[28] Productivity and profits increase, but so do fatigue, stress, and injuries for workers, undermining their original vision of a "good job."

Perhaps the workers believe in the rating system and internalize the values to which they imagine it responds—punctuality, stamina, attention to detail. Perhaps they see and judge themselves and others by the game metrics. Or perhaps they see the emperor's ass quite clearly—but change their behavior anyway because their livelihoods depend on it. Either way, the result is a tale as old as time: the boss gains, and the worker loses.

It is clear that the forces of capital have found uses for game thinking. But, as Nguyen is careful to point out, a shadowy cabal of plotters' deliberate use of game design strategies to control people is the exception, not the rule, of value capture.[29] Deliberate or calculated intervention is not a prerequisite for value capture; rather, it requires only an environment or incentive structure that encourages excess value clarity.

For example, we can imagine ourselves participating in good faith conversations on a new social media platform about a particular social issue. This platform is structured, of course, by designers employed by the company owners, who build and manage algorithms that direct the traffic of posts and encourage consumer engagement. As we talk on this platform, its features begin to affect our behavior: simpler takes attract comments and shares, affecting what people say on the platform. The tech-company owners get the lion's share of revenue generated by the site's traffic, driven by our conversations, and a small number of site participants get the lion's share of attention directed by the activity on the platform. An elite emerges.

It would be a mistake, however, to understand everything that happens on the platform as a process orchestrated by the elites. They are its *results*, like the platform's unequal distribution of profit and attention itself. Elites *do* often make the environment worse and block solutions, but to blame the problem of elite capture entirely on their moral successes and failures is to confuse effect for cause. The true problem lies in the system itself, the built environment and rules of interaction that produced the elites in the first place.

In games, there are clear boundaries of power between the designers and the players. The designers experience a wide scope of choice, while the choices they make become fixed features of the game for players. Gamers enter an environment and experience the rules of interaction and basic incentives laid out for them by the designers, without themselves having a say in any of these.

This environment is not so different from the real world as it might seem. As Carter G. Woodson realized, many of our decisions are shaped by decisions that someone with more power made before us. The whole social structure affects how institutional systems, like schools, function. In turn, those institutional systems exert power over the interactions that take place within them—conversations, lectures, relationships.

A game environment responds to most players in similar ways: they encounter the same rules, costs, and incentives. The social environment responds differently to different people, as David Lewis's conversation between master and slave reminds us. The paper in which Lewis invokes this conversation, called "Scorekeeping in a Language Game," concerns itself with the way background rules combine with our previous decisions to tell us what action makes sense for us to take at a specific juncture. Lewis uses baseball as an example to show how clear this is in a game context: whether the batter gets to walk to first base has to do with both the rules of the sport (including about how many balls any pitcher can throw before a batter walks) and how things have gone up until now (how many balls this pitcher has thrown on this particular at-bat).[30] But his earlier example of the master inventing rules for the slave on the fly more accurately describes many social interactions. After all, life is not nearly as fair as baseball.

As we saw in chapter 1, sufficiently powerful people and institutions are able to change, reconstruct, and ignore the rules of the game at will. While this works in different ways in different kinds of interactions and different parts of society, let's start where most of us hope to start our day: in a home. Under capitalism, an environment in which housing is commodified, whether someone has as an actionable choice to be housed or not depends greatly on the rules and rule-like actions of a small group of elites: individual landlords, corporate landlords, the police, and the data agencies that traffic information between these groups.[31] Elites have captured the means of maintaining shelter, so they set the rules by which the rest of us succeed or fail to win shelter.

What about the rest of your day? If you engage in any kind of economic activity whatsoever, then you are involved in some way with productive processes. And so, we encounter a familiar story of elite capture that ain't broke: the capitalists have captured the means of production. This is a familiar idea, but it is worth noting how, in doing so, they've also effectively captured huge swaths of human experience.

The social control held by capitalists in the production process claims as much of a worker's life and experience as employers can manage. Employers, not state governments, serve as the functional arbiters of workers' rights to freedoms of association and speech during the majority of their waking hours.[32] Sociologist Arlie Hochschild's much-belabored concept of "emotional labor" was originally a comment on the control bosses assert over the emotional expression of workers.[33] And, of course, elites structure workers' own access to the products that they spend so much time producing under their rules; working in health care doesn't guarantee you can afford your own.

Formal political structures are also famously plagued by elite capture. In a dismayingly literal fashion, laws are increasingly made by the powerful: in the United States, groups representing the interests of multibillion-dollar corporations, such as the American Legislative Exchange Council, write legislation that protects their interests, including bills that have criminalized protest against oil and gas infrastructure under the guise of "national security."[34]

Government regulators and courts, supposedly empowered to reign in the excesses of capitalists, often end up integrated into their profit-making plans instead—a process economists have helpfully termed "regulatory capture."[35]

Regulatory capture has dire consequences. In Nigeria, for instance, the relative power of regulation versus profit is so low that oil companies have either evaded regulatory fines or simply priced them into their business plans. A high-profile struggle of Ogoni people in 1993 to hold Shell accountable brought international attention to the ecological crisis in the Niger Delta caused by Shell's practices.[36] Despite the attention, Shell's behavior remained unchanged; in fact, researchers Enegide Chinedu and Chukwuma Kelechukwu Chukwuemeka found that oil spill incidents actually *increased* in the years after the controversy.[37]

Media (a field dominated by conglomerates in which advertising, public relations, and branding mingle with civic, social, artistic, and educational functions) are organized around attention and engagement. While "in the final analysis" these are often convertible into capital, many individuals feel that media creates a haven where we can escape some of the constraints that define our work lives and political experiences.[38] But, as with the material economy, those atop the attention economy exert the most influence over how the critical resources of attention and engagement are distributed.

Influential elites' (including social media "influencers") decisions about where to invest time or capital have outsize social effects that show up as fixed features of others' interactions. Their posts get engagement and attention, structuring which topics are trending, who Twitter's "main character" is for the day, and thus which topics are on the conversational agenda. When the rest of us make choices about what to watch or read or respond to, we're mostly making choices in an environment shaped by elites.

Does all of this sound familiar? Indeed it should after chapter 2. The genius of Carter G. Woodson was to see and articulate this pattern of elite capture in a history that began long before Twitter. Woodson put it plainly: "The so-called modern education, with all its defects, however, does others so much more good than it does the Negro, because it has been worked out in conformity to the needs of those who have enslaved and oppressed weaker peoples."[39] Woodson was analyzing how the rules of social interaction set by those in the "master" role in society affected the basic architecture of education, including the common ground of conversations held in classrooms.

It's bigger than conversation. Whole territories of social life have been captured by those at the top. This capture is built into the rules of engagement that result from colonial ownership. Capital accumulation is highly game-like in the clarity of its incentive structure, and its elite players have for several centuries been transforming the world so that more and more aspects of it become playable by the rules of capitalism. Most people end up playing along perforce, because the world as we find it at the level of individual interactions is an environment stocked with choices, penalties, and potential rewards that make sense in capitalist terms.

Whether it is a human manager or an Uber driver-rating algorithm telling the worker they should smile at the customer, the smile becomes an action that now makes sense for them to take, because playing along is the safest strategy for obtaining her objective—a paycheck.

Whether an oil-industry regulator accepts a bribe to look the other way or assiduously builds a fine and fee structure they know is bound to fail, they too are playing along.

Whether a student omits their own history from their paper because they believe the professor who said that Black people have no important history, or because they simply observe that the successful students always pick topics from white history, or because they can't find any books on Black history, they too are playing for the short-term win for themselves, following rules set down by someone else.

The game objective may be viscerally and irreducibly personal for each player—self-esteem, security, life itself—but the rules and the context that determine which actions make sense have been created by others who benefit from the outcome of those rigged systems.

The so-called common ground has been captured in the same way that oil regulatory infrastructures have. It is, after all, just "public information": things we treat as true together.

We use public information to do things—to communicate, yes, but also to do everything else that we do together.[40] As philosophers Kristie Dotson and Saray Ayala explain, it's a structure not so much of *beliefs*, but of "common epistemic resources" and "affordances": stuff built into the social environment that we can use to act together.[41] We act as if the information in the common ground is true, in the main, for much the same reason that we walk on sidewalks—it's easiest, and that's what it's there for.

Understood this way, common ground is just the informational aspect of the social environment that we build and rebuild with words and deeds. And when we successfully challenge the common ground, we are changing the social environment itself.[42]

3

Being in the Room

"In accepting to be led like sheep, European workers were perpetuating their own enslavement to the capitalists. . . . They failed to exercise any independent judgment on the great issues of war and peace, and therefore ended up by slaughtering not only colonial peoples but also themselves."
—Walter Rodney, *How Europe Underdeveloped Africa*[1]

"Without any doubt, underestimation of the cultural values of African peoples, based upon racist feelings and upon the intention of perpetuating foreign exploitation of Africans, has done much harm to Africa. But in the face of the vital need for progress, the following attitudes or behaviors will be no less harmful to Africa; indiscriminate compliments; systematic exaltation of virtues without condemning faults; blind acceptance of the values of the culture, without considering what presently or potentially regressive elements it contains; confusion between what is the expression of an objective and material

historical reality and what appears to be a creation of the mind or the product of a peculiar temperament."
                            —Amílcar Cabral, *Return to the Source*[2]

The last chapter may have been frustrating: all this talk about social structure, but what about our choices? Doesn't it matter how I decide to play the games life presents me? Aren't I free to respect the people around me, even if society says I should not—and aren't I to blame for my failures to do so, even if society encouraged those failures? How can elites have captured *everything*? And if they have, what's left? How can we possibly win in a world so thoroughly rigged and bought?

Yes, some forms of resistance to a rigged game are dead ends. They are anticipated by the designers, or pushback against the machinery leads only to marginal improvement, or resistance makes it worse.

We *can* do more than resist. We can do better. But before we can have a meaningful discussions about such tactics, it's really crucial to pay attention to what room the discussion is happening in.

What about right now? How did you and I get to be here, interacting across this page?

I could, after all, like many other people in the world, have simply read and thought about all of these issues on my own. I could even have spoken to my friends and colleagues about them. But that would not give me the power to speak to *you*.

According to the rules of racial capitalism, very few of the thousands or millions of people in the world who have some kind of insight into elite capture have the ability to enter a room where you, my reader, are available and open to listen to their thoughts. Maybe this book and the thoughts it contains are in the room with you only because of those rules. But maybe it's here with you in spite of them. Maybe the rules don't constrain us quite as much as I've suggested.

Activist and revolutionary Lilica Boal understood the difference between the rules that tell us who we are supposed to be and the actual choices we have when we act. After all, she was the sort of person who occasionally went off script, and who went into rooms she was not supposed to be in.

In June of 1961, the young Cape Verdean student was in a room she definitely was not supposed to be in: a Spanish prison.

Lilica should have known better. She was born in 1934 in the city of Tarrafal on the Cape Verdean island of Santiago, two years before the Portuguese Empire had built the Colónia Penal no Tarrafal (penal colony in Tarrafal), which housed antifascist dissidents to Portugal's dictatorial regime. The Boals were relatively well off for Cape Verdeans, especially for Black Cape Verdeans: in addition to owning property, her parents were merchants, and the penal colony was one of their customers.

Such middle-class status was not particularly easy to reach. For centuries, Portuguese colonial officials had conspired with plantation owners to prevent the islander Cape Verdeans from owning any nautical vessels, thus excluding the population from the food security and economic opportunities of the archipelago's considerable marine resources. This management was intimately tied to the empire's centuries-long use of the islands as a stopover point in the transatlantic slave trade, but also its persistent use of these islands as a containment area for exiled criminals, political deportees, and mutinous soldiers. For the Portuguese Empire, Cape Verde was, itself, a gulag.[3]

Lilica remembers watching trucks full of prisoners arrive to the prison, with panes installed to prevent anyone on the outside from seeing who was imprisoned inside of them. No one spoke of it, but everyone noticed: a constant warning about the price of defying the empire.[4]

Another linked episode from Lilica's childhood loomed large in her memory: the devastating famines of the 1940s, which claimed over forty-five thousand lives.[5] They were the latest in a succession of famines, which had been constant in Cape Verde over the centuries. These periods of extreme food scarcity were often blamed on droughts, but the real story was more complex, with wholly man-made elements. Low food production on the land was the result of soil depletion and erosion, which had been caused by centuries of unsustainable farming and herding practices on the island's plantations.[6] In addition to their outright subjugation, the vulnerability of Cape Verdeans to the problems on the farms was wildly exacerbated by the colonial prohibition on owning ships, which could have been used to supplement crops with seafood.[7]

For centuries, that man-made vulnerability to famine wrapped itself tightly around the island's racial hierarchy. At the top of the hierarchy were the few peninsular-born "super white" *brancos* (typically the governor, chief military officers, and top clergy). Just below them were the *brancos da terra*, or island-born whites, led by the old white *morgado* families who had been granted estates by the Portuguese crown. These landed proprietors were less than 5 percent of the population of the islands but owned and controlled virtually all of its arable land. Below these were mixed-race *pardos*, who were sometimes enslaved but often free, and were permitted some branco privileges, including European dress. At the bottom were the Black *pretos*. Enslaved pretos were often forced to work six days a week, leaving only one for the production of their own food; free pretos were forced into sharecropping arrangements that were not altogether dissimilar from outright slavery. Even after the abolition of slavery in 1864, which upended one crucial legal basis for this social structure, death from famine continued to correlate with the social status built by this hierarchy: brancos and pardos were likelier to own fruit trees and gardens, or valuables that they could sell for food when crisis struck—and, every few decades, it did.[8]

If they had been provided food aid from abroad, Cape Verdeans could possibly have survived even both of these problems, but by the 1940s the ruling Portuguese Empire had entered into what historian Alexander Keese calls "a dynamic of maximum exploitation of colonial populations." Their approach, which coupled indifference to colonial suffering with a lack of investment in basic infrastructure or administrative capacity, all but ensured that there would be plenty of suffering to go around.[9] Lilica recalls one occasion in which the Portuguese colonial administration responded to a plea for help from the governor of Cape Verde. They promptly sent money to the islands—to expand Tarrafal's cemetery.[10]

Lilica remembers much more: the bodies in the streets of those who had starved to death, the pots of food her family made to feed those around them. But she also remembers the remove she and the families of the prison guards felt from the struggle that surrounded them.[11] This changed when her family got a visit from a white Portuguese family.

Luís Alves de Carvalho and Dona Herculana were as out of place in Tarrafal as Lilica Boal would eventually be in Lisbon. The family was from Porto, a major city in Portugal, where Luís worked as a stockbroker. The draw of the small city of Tarrafal was not business opportunity, but the prison: it housed their antifascist teenage son, Guilherme da Costa Carvalho.[12]

The city of Tarrafal had neither a hotel nor even a restaurant. But a mutual business partner had told Luis about Lilica's family, who accepted the couple into their home. The Portuguese couple used the opportunity to visit with their son and his antifascist comrades.

Some time after the couple returned to Portugal, Lilica got the rare opportunity to enroll in college in Lisbon. There, they became Lilica's second family. When Guilherme was transferred out of Tarrafal to a prison in Portugal, she would go to the prison in Peniche to visit him.[13]

Partially through these visits, Lilica began to meet more and more leftists in Portugal. In addition to the incarcerated antifascists she met and heard of via her visits with Guilherme, the Portuguese couple introduced her to members of the Portuguese Communist Party like Virgínia Moura and Maria Cal Brandão, and involved the families of political prisoners in family get-togethers.[14] Later on, Lilica met and married her husband, Manuel Boal, a medical student from Angola, and their first daughter Sara was born soon after.

Perhaps the most important of these meetings came in 1960, when Lilica moved to Lisbon to spend time with the Casa dos Estudantes do Império (CEI; house of students of the empire). There, students in Lisbon from Angola, Mozambique, São Tomé, and Guinea-Bissau—Portugal's African colonies—all met to discuss the situations in their various countries and decide what contribution they could make. They figured that whatever they were going to do, they weren't going to do it in Lisbon. So they resolved to smuggle themselves out of the country and back to their respective homelands—the "flight to the fight." This was a particularly difficult decision for Lilica and Manuel, whose daughter was only seventeen months old, but the couple decided to send Sara to Lilica's mother in Tarrafal and join the charge.

Lilica and Manuel packed what belongings they could fit into a ten-pound suitcase and took off with other students they knew from the CEI. They made it to the border with Spain, bribing their way onto a small smuggling boat, but were caught and spent two days in a Spanish prison. There, Portuguese police asked their Spanish counterparts to turn them over to Portuguese authorities, but the Conselho Ecumenico das Igrejas (ecumenical council of churches) pressured the Spanish authorities into letting them continue on toward France. The couple and their comrades eventually made it to Germany, where they met a plane sent by the prime minister of Ghana, Kwame Nkrumah, that ferried the students to that country.[15]

But they did. Lilica went on to play an important role in Cape Verde and Guinea-Bissau's revolutionary struggle against the Portuguese Empire and its subsequent nation-building project, helping both to plan military strategy and to develop their approaches to education and solidarity-based international relations.[16]

Deference Politics

The history of Cape Verde and Guinea-Bissau and the deep racial, gender, class, religious, and other divisions cleaving the peoples of those places apart from each other makes it hard to understand how there was revolutionary struggle there at all, much less a successful one. The rules of social interaction would seem to rule out any kind of workable solidarity. Indeed, if Lilica had stuck to the social script, it's hard to see how she would have ended up in something like the PAIGC at all, much less in so pivotal of a role.

But the point of the last chapter was not that we are powerless in the face of history and social structure. It was, rather, to clarify how much of the game has already been played by the time society hands us the controller. Nonetheless, we can and do retain meaningful power and responsibility, even inside the mechanics of a game that is so powerfully rigged.

One way of responding to this rigged game is to focus on where we're at already. History has built the rooms around us; we find ourselves in places, and with people, resources, and incentives, that we did not choose.

The first rules we learn to follow are the ones that apply to the room we are in. The powers that be have decided those rules, including where the resources are and who is granted access to them. As we saw in the previous chapter, they even set the rules for how the environment responds to our actions, and frequently the environment is hostile. But they don't actually control, directly, what our actions are. So there is an opportunity here, of a sort.

When it comes to our interpersonal interactions inside the rooms of our daily lives, we can act on the basis of rules that we actively agree to—the emperor's rules be damned. We may not be able to control how the room reacts to our speech, but we *can* speak. We can also choose not to speak, to invite someone else in the room to speak, or to follow their lead.

These are the kinds of opportunities seized on by deference politics, which considers it a step toward justice to the modify interpersonal interactions in compliance with the perceived wishes of the marginalized. While the deference perspective isn't entirely off base, it is potentially limiting and misleading. In such a game, it is much trickier than we realize to avoid moves that intensify elite capture and other oppressive aspects of our social structure—even when we use strategies that correctly identify the distribution of power in the room we're in.

After all, some rooms have outsize power and influence: the White House Situation Room, the newsroom, the bargaining table, the conference room. Being in one of *these* rooms means that our words and actions affect institutions and broader social dynamics outside of it. To be in such a room is itself a kind of social advantage, often gained by way of some prior social advantage.

A prime example of deference politics is the call to "listen to the most affected" or "center the most marginalized," now ubiquitous in many academic and activist circles. These calls have never sat well with me. In my experience as an academic and organizer, when people have said they needed to "listen to the most affected," it wasn't usually because they intended to set up Skype calls to refugee camps or to collaborate with houseless people. Acting on this conception of "centering the most marginalized" would require a different approach entirely, in a world where 1.6 billion people live in inadequate housing (slum conditions) and 100 million are unhoused, a full third of the human population does not have reliable drinking water, and the intersections of food, energy, and water insecurity with the climate crisis have already displaced 8.5 million people in South Asia alone, while threatening to displace tens of millions more.[17] Such a stance would require, at a minimum, that one leave the room.

Instead, "centering the most marginalized" in my experience has usually meant handing conversational authority and attentional goods to whoever is already in the room and appears to fit a social category associated with some form of oppression—regardless of what they have or have not actually experienced, or what they do or do not actually know about the matter at hand. Even in rooms where stakes have been high—where potential researchers were discussing how to understand a social phenomenon, where activists were deciding what to target—the rules of deference have often meant that the conversation stayed in the room, while the people most affected by it stayed outside.

This particular politics of deference emerged out of a theoretical orientation called standpoint epistemology, which became popular in feminist circles in the 1970s and has continued to contribute to the thinking of many activists and academics since.[18] Standpoint epistemology comprises three seemingly innocuous ideas:

1) knowledge is socially situated,

2) marginalized people have some advantages in gaining some forms of knowledge, and

3) research programs (and other areas of human activity) ought to reflect these facts.

These ideas should go down easy. As Liam Kofi Bright argues, any serious empiricist philosophy would entail all three of these points.[19] Moreover, they are politically important: they point to the value of lived experience and the knowledge that comes from it. At face value, a commitment to these ideas should help us resist and contain elite capture. They should provide a basis for respecting knowledge that the institutions of the world otherwise want to discredit.

But the devil is in the details. The common approaches to putting these abstract ideas into practice emphasize deference to others in conversational contexts, in an effort to fix the distribution of attention: they ask that we pass the mic, believe marginalized people, and give offerings.

The motivation is admirable, and these actions themselves are often good ideas, as far as they go. But aside from involving attitudes and interpersonal dynamics, oppression—racism, ableism, xenophobia, patriarchy, and so forth—also have serious *material* consequences. These structures of injustice decide who has reliable access to basic interpersonal security, housing, health care, water, and energy. All of these consequences of bigotry, from the attitudinal to the material, have to be dealt with if we are to address oppression.

The politics of deference focuses on the consequences that are likeliest to show up in the rooms where elites do most of their interacting: classrooms, boardrooms, political parties. As a result, we seem to end up with far more, and more specific, practical advice about how to, say, allocate tasks at a committee meeting than how to keep people alive.

Deference as a default political orientation can work counter to marginalized groups' interests. We are surrounded by a discourse that locates attentional injustice in the selection of spokespeople and book lists taken to represent the marginalized, rather than focusing on the actions of the corporations and algorithms that much more powerfully distribute attention. This discourse ultimately participates in the weaponization of attention in the service of marginalization. It directs what little attentional power we can control at symbolic sites of power rather than at the root political issues that explain why everything is so fucked up.

A trip down memory lane provides a powerful example of both the opportunities and limitations of the deferential approach. In 2007, Barack Obama was on the campaign trail for the US presidency. Obama had just lost two of the first three primary contests to Hillary Clinton. He gave a speech to a small crowd in Greenwood, South Carolina, looking exhausted and disheartened. Suddenly, an attendee named Edith S. Childs called out words of encouragement: "Fired up, ready to go!" People around her repeated the chant, and the energy in the crowd crescendoed. After a newly energized Barack Obama crushed Clinton in the South Carolina primary, those five words became a slogan of the campaign that carried the young upstart into the White House.[20]

Two years later, President Barack Obama went back out on the speaking trail—this time to Minneapolis, Minnesota, in defense of his fight to expand access to health care. President Obama explained that he "always believed that change doesn't come from the top down; it comes from the bottom up. . . . It begins with you sharing your stories, fighting for something better."[21] But what does change coming from the "bottom up" mean, in this context? The president was remarkably explicit: "[I]t goes to show you how one voice can change a room. And if it changes a room, it can change a city. And if it can change a city, it can change a state. And if it can change a state, it can change a nation. If it change[s] the nation, it can change the world." In other words, the president held forth a model of change flowing through approved channels and hierarchies atop which, ultimately, he stood.

We tend to be on our guard for this kind of cynical use of "bottom up" thinking by elites when we deal with politicians and formal, electoral politics. But, as political theorist

Jo Freeman has argued, our own rooms are not free of this phenomenon.[22] According to Freeman, any group of people interacting with each other will structure itself in some way or other, whether consciously or unconsciously, leaving only the question of how that resulting structure distributes resources, responsibilities, attention, and power.

Elites from marginalized groups can benefit from deference in ways that are at least compatible with social progress, especially if we take the right actions afterward. But treating such elites' interests as necessarily or even presumptively aligned with the broader group's interests involves a political naivete we cannot afford. In this context, confusion about elite interests functions as a form of racial Reaganomics: a strategy reliant on fantasies about the exchange rate between the attention economy and the material economy.

We need to fix the social structure itself—the rooms we interact in, and the house they make up. Deference, as a strategy, bears at best a tenuous relationship to this goal.

The View from Inside the Room

To say what's wrong with the popular, deferential applications of standpoint epistemology, we need to understand what makes it popular. First, a cynical answer: deference to figures from oppressed communities is a performance that sanitizes, apologizes for, or simply distracts from the fact that the deferrer has enough "in the room" privilege for their "lifting up" of a perspective to be of consequence—to reflect well on *them*.

In her influential essay "The Tyranny of Structureless-ness," Freeman notes that "structurelessness" in the women's liberation movement did not resolve the problem of unequal and unfair distributions of power; instead, it provided a mask behind which informal networks of well-positioned elites could hide their outsize influence on the culture and activities of the group.[23]

Unlike structurelessness, deference politics doesn't mask its distributive consequences. Visible performance of a deferential act of "passing the mic" or "stepping back" in order to give attention or space to another person does tend to redistribute short-term attention, as promised. But deference politics can still mask essential power relations, especially when we consider the performance in the context of the people who aren't in the room at all. For instance, one white person giving the mic to the specific person of color in the room can obscure both the overall power dynamics of the room and the whole room's relationship to the broader category of "people of color" that a particular comrade is taken to represent.

It would be reasonable to assume that most of those who practice standpoint epistemology deferentially do so for the right reasons, and that they trust the people they share the room with to help them find the proper practical expression of their joint moral commitments. Indeed, we don't need to attribute bad faith to all or even most of those who practice deferential politics to explain the phenomenon.

Bad roommates aren't the problem, for the same reason that being a good roommate isn't the solution: the problem is that we are still trapped in the room. If we want better politics, we have to challenge how those rooms are put together, the security system that controls access to them, and the rules that dictate what happens in them.

For illustration, we can return to the question of how you came to read this book—how it is that you and I are interacting through this text, right now. To do so, we have to consider the layers of history, politics, and geography that made its writing possible.

Many aspects of our social system serve as filtering mechanisms, determining which interactions happen and between whom, and thus, what social patterns people are in a position to observe. For the majority of the twentieth century, the US immigration quota system made legal immigration with a path to citizenship available almost exclusively to Europeans (earning Adolf Hitler's regard as the world "leader in developing explicitly racist policies of nationality and immigration," in the words of legal scholar James Q. Whitman).[24]

But the 1965 Immigration and Nationality Act opened up immigration possibilities to more people, with a preference for "skilled labor." My family migrated from Nigeria to the United States under these auspices, becoming part of the Nigerian American community that makes up one of the country's most successful immigrant populations. What no one mentions, of course, is that the 112,000 or so Nigerian Americans with advanced degrees are utterly dwarfed by the 82 million Nigerians who live on less than a dollar a day.

The selectivity of US immigration law helps explain the rates of educational attainment in the Nigerian diasporic community that raised me, which in turn helps explain the wealth, class advantages, and cultural expectations that fueled my own educational development.[25]

The class advantages I grew up with help explain which rooms I was educated and socialized in during elementary and middle school, which in turn help explain my entry into the exclusive Advanced Placement and honors classes in high school, while others from more disadvantaged backgrounds were routed through remedial courses. This in turn helps explain my access to higher education, which involved admission to schools from which others were rejected, and so on.

Indeed, the education system is a ready and uncommonly explicit example of selection processes. This is the trajectory that explains why *my* thoughts on elite capture were originally accepted and published as an article in *The Philosopher,*[26] and why I have the resources now to write a whole book that even nonphilosophers might read. It's a case in point of what sociological researchers call "cumulative advantage" or the "Matthew effect": the people who were successful yesterday are likeliest to get today's rewards, which makes them yet more likely to get tomorrow's as well.[27]

With these selections in view, it is easy to see how this deferential form of standpoint epistemology contributes to elite capture at scale. The higher the form of education, the narrower the social experience. Some students are pipelined to PhDs, while others are pipelined to prisons—and the very oppressive structures we aim to challenge largely explain who goes where. Deferential ways of dealing with identity can easily inherit the distortions caused by these selection processes.

But it's equally easy to see locally—in *this* room, in *this* social space, in *this* conversation—why deference seems to make sense. It may be an improvement on the epistemic procedure that preceded it. The Black person in the elite room may well be better positioned than non-Black people in this space to think about policing and incarceration. So, if we have to listen to one person, perhaps it's better that it be a Black person, even an affluent and privileged Black person, than the affluent and privileged white person who would otherwise have dominated the discussion. Put another way, deference can often seem like the best we can do in the face of what we take to be the fixed facts about the room and its purpose, and who's in it.

But these are the last facts we should want to hold fixed. And if our aim is simply to do better than the epistemic norms that we've inherited from a history of explicit global apartheid, that is an awfully low bar to set.

The facts that explain *who* ends up in *what* room shape our world much more powerfully than the squabbles for comparative prestige between people who have already made it inside. And when the conversation is about social justice, the social mechanisms that determine who gets into the room are often exactly what needs to change—for example, the fact that incarcerated people cannot participate in academic discussions about freedom is intimately related to the fact that they are physically locked in cages.

Still, deference does have attractive qualities. After all, the people in powerful rooms, to whom others defer, may be "elites" relative to the larger group they represent, but disadvantaged relative to the other people in the rooms with them.

Our sense of ourselves—and the patterns of deference we tend to fit to our standpoint epistemological commitments—often foregrounds the ways in which we are marginalized, rather than the ways we are not. A privileged person in an absolute sense (a person belonging to, say, the half of the world that has secure access to "basic needs") may nevertheless experience themselves consistently on the low end of the power dynamics of their immediate social world. The rooms we are in, which is to say the social dynamics we actually experience, play a central part in developing and refining our political subjectivity and our sense of ourselves.

Deference responds to real, morally weighty experiences of being put down, ignored, sidelined, silenced. The fact that others have graver problems does not legitimate bigotry toward the relatively advantaged.

People are—and ought to be—vying for respect, dignity, and some measure of recognition alongside policy reforms and material redistribution. We all deserve these attentional goods, which are often denied, even to the "elites" of marginalized and stigmatized groups. Moreover, distributions of respect and care can be won and lost collectively; there is *some* connection between the inside of the room and the outside. The deference interpretation of standpoint epistemology thus has an important non-epistemic appeal to such elites: it intervenes directly in morally consequential practices of giving attention and respect.

This focus on one's own relative marginalization is especially easy to cultivate when exposure to people below us in the relevant hierarchies is controlled or prevented, which is, after all, a great deal of what rooms do. This foregrounding of the personal happens for a reason that is entirely compatible with the ethos of "standpoint epistemology" and valuing lived experience. Our personal emphasis on the ways we are marginalized often matches the world *as we have experienced it*. And such a focus may be in some ways convenient for the practitioners of deference epistemology. Nonetheless, I still think that the cynical view does them too little credit. Many who practice deference epistemology are simply doing the best they can.

However, this same phenomenon also illustrates how the strength of standpoint epistemology, its recognition of the importance of perspective, becomes its weakness when flattened into deference politics. From a structural perspective, the rooms we *don't* enter, the experiences we *don't* have (and the reasons we are able to avoid them) might have more to teach us about the world and our place in it than anything said inside. If so, the deferential approach to standpoint epistemology actually *prevents* "centering" or even hearing from the most marginalized, since it focuses us on the interactions inside the rooms we occupy, rather than calling us to account for the interactions we needn't and typically don't have.

For those who are deferred to, the performance of deference can supercharge group-undermining norms.

In her book *Conflict Is Not Abuse*, activist writer and scholar Sarah Schulman makes a provocative observation about the psychological effects of both trauma and felt superiority: while these often come about for different reasons and have very different moral statuses, they result in similar behavioral patterns. Chief among these are misrepresenting the stakes of conflict (often by overstating harm) and representing others' independence as a hostile threat (for example, calling out failures to "center" the right topics or people). These behaviors, whatever their causal history, have corrosive effects, especially when a community's norms magnify or multiply rather than constrain or metabolize them.

For those who defer, the habit can supercharge moral cowardice, as the norms of deference provide social cover for the abdication of responsibility. It displaces onto individual heroes, a hero class, or a mythicized past the work that is ours to do in the present. Their perspective may be clearer on this or that specific matter, but their overall point of view isn't any less particular or constrained by history than ours. More importantly, deference places the accountability that is all of ours to bear onto select people—and, more often than not, a sanitized and thoroughly fictional caricature of them.

Deference to collectives or their culture has many of the same risks as deference to marginalized individual. PAIGC militant Amílcar Cabral affirmed the need to respond to centuries of anti-Black racism and the widespread assumptions about the inferiority of African history and culture. He, of course, denied that anything like a single African culture existed. But even if it did, reference to it would not answer questions about how we ought to behave and organize ourselves politically, since "all culture is composed of essential and secondary elements, of strengths and weaknesses, of virtues and failings, of positive and negative aspects, of factors of progress and factors of stagnation or regression." He went as far as to insist that "blind acceptance of the values of the culture, without considering what presently or potentially regressive elements it contains" would be "no less harmful to Africa" than racist underestimation of African culture had been.[28]

The same tactics of deference that insulate us from criticism and disagreement insulate us from connection and transformation. They prevent us from engaging empathetically and authentically with the struggles of other people—a prerequisite of coalitional politics.

Moreover, as identities become more and more fine grained and disagreements sharper, we come to realize that "coalitional politics" (understood as struggle across difference) is, simply, politics. Thus, the deferential orientation, like that fragmentation of political collectivity it enables, is ultimately anti-political.

To opt for deference, rather than interdependence, may soothe short-term psychological wounds. But it does so at a steep cost: it may undermine the goals that motivated the project—and it entrenches a politics that does not serve those fighting for freedom over privilege, for collective liberation over mere parochial advantage.

Better Blueprints

Deference politics is right about the *what*: it does in fact matter that we pay attention to lived experiences, and it is politically important that we pay attention to difference. But it is wrong about the *how*, because the more we focus on changing our norms of interactions to ones that locally and cosmetically elevate the voices and perspectives *in* the room, the harder it becomes to change the world *outside* of the room.

As philosopher C. Thi Nguyen reminded us in the last chapter, the power of the system is that of the game designer. It builds our social, economic, cultural, and even attentional environment in ways that get us to follow its game plan.

In the speech I quoted at the beginning of this chapter, Amílcar Cabral explains another important aspect of this systemic control: "[I]mperialist domination . . . for its own security, requires cultural oppression and the attempt at direct or indirect liquidation of the essential elements of the culture of the dominated people." Culture, for Cabral, is our collective ability to design and organize our own lives, and be the engines of our own history—an ability that conflicts directly with the aims of imperialists to be the ones doing the designing and controlling. This is why, "whatever may be the material aspects of this domination," imperialist domination can survive "only by the permanent, organized repression of the cultural life of the people concerned."[29]

This, above all, illustrates the key problem with deference: it focuses the very capacity that we have to reconstruct the whole house to the specific rooms that have already been built for us. It advertises itself as deferring to marginalized voices and perspectives, but in conceding so much creative space to the blueprint of society, it is perhaps better understood as deference to the built structure of society.

I am arguing here for another approach—one that concedes that we have to start with the interactions that we have most control over, but that keeps in view the point of changing how those interactions go: to rebuild the whole of society, not just our interactions. Rooting ourselves here thus gives us a *constructive* politics.

A constructive politics pursues specific goals or end results, rather than aiming to avoid "complicity" in injustices that we assume will mostly persist anyway. If it's "epistemology" or knowledge practices we're concerned about, then a constructive politics focuses on institutions and practices of information gathering that are strategically useful for challenging social injustices themselves, not just the symptoms manifest in the room we happen to be in today.

In general, a constructive politics is one that engages directly in the task of redistributing social resources and powe,r rather than pursuing intermediary goals cashed out in symbols.

This is a demanding approach. It asks that we swim upstream, that we be accountable and responsive to people who aren't yet in the room, and that we build the kinds of rooms in which we can sit together, rather than merely seek to navigate more gracefully the rooms history has built for us.

The task of rebuilding the world is demanding—and it's constructive politics, not deferential politics, that brings these demands together.

4

Building a New House

"Resistance is the following: to destroy something, in order to build something else. That's what resistance is. What do we want to destroy on our land? The colonial domination of the Portuguese soldiers. Just that by itself? No—at the same time, we don't want any other time of colonial domination on our land, or any other kind of foreign domination. We want our people to determine their own destiny, through their children, in Guinea and Cape Verde. This is our primary objective."

—Amílcar Cabral, *Análise de Alguns Tipos de Resistência*[1]

Paulo Freire had a very hungry childhood.

Still, it could have been worse. Freire was born in Recife, Brazil, in 1921—a place he would later call "the center of one of the most extreme situations of poverty and underdevelopment in the Third World."[2] The Freires were a temporarily precarized middle-class family whose normal economic security was upset by the exceptional circumstances of the Great

85

Depression.[3] As such, Paulo and his siblings were "connective kids," socially linked with both the well-off and the poor.

But the hunger that bound him by common experience to the children from the "poor outskirts of town" did not do so without qualification: he and his siblings were still "people from another world who happened to fall accidentally into their world."[4] While hunger arrived to his family "unannounced and unauthorized, making itself at home without an end in sight," it arrived to a living room with a piano and a household led by a man who wore a necktie to work—markers of class status that the Freires clung to for dear life.

Perhaps as a result, hunger came and went from their family before it could have the consequences that it had for millions of the working-class Brazilians in the "other world" that the Freire kids chanced upon. For many of these childhood friends, legs, arms, and fingers had been rendered thin and brittle, eyes had retreated into sockets—signs of persistent malnutrition, the kind of hunger that brought a moving truck instead of a suitcase.

Even so, Paulo never forgot. During his six years of exile, having fled the Brazilian military dictatorship that took power via a US-backed coup in 1964, he documented these experiences in what would become his most influential book, *Pedagogy of the Oppressed*.[5] The book introduces key ideas, including his criticism of what he called the banking model of education, in which teachers view poor students as passive, empty receptacles to be filled with the information they, the teachers, possess.[6]

This model, and the unchanging roles of the conferring teacher and receptive student that it assumes, are obstacles to be overcome. In the education of children and adults alike, the banking model attempts to create "automatons" who neither think nor act for themselves—and to prevent *conscientização* (critical consciousness), the mutually humanizing relationship between those from "oppressed" and "oppressor" backgrounds that results from a mutually liberatory education.[7]

Conscientização aims at the opposite of elite capture. While both elite capture and conscientização bring elites and non-elites together, elite capture perpetuates and exploits the divide by conscripting non-elites into the service of elites' interests; conscientização, on the other hand, aims to pursue the kind of mutually liberatory political project that would eliminate the distinction between elites and non-elites entirely.

This liberatory approach to education, Paulo argued, would begin by acknowledging the knowledge students and teachers both bring into any situation. But it would end with the transformation of the social relations that relied on their "education" into life as cogs in someone else's machine in the first place—that is, society itself. So he got to work, starting in the spaces to which he had access and in which he had power: classrooms.

Rebuild the House: Lilica, Paulo, and the PAIGC

The story of our global political system—the big house in which we all occupy rooms—begins with the explorations and conquests of the Portuguese Empire. In the previous chapter, we saw how Lilica Boal made a daring escape from the school room she was in. The struggle she left to join was the one taking place against the Portuguese Empire.

Long before Christopher Columbus set sail under the Spanish flag in 1492—the same year that the year the Christian powers finally removed the last Muslim dynasty from the Iberian Peninsula (completing the so-called Reconquista)—Portugal had long been hard at work building the colonies and trade relationships that would produce the transatlantic slave trade and thereby the modern world economy.[8]

Portuguese explorers sailed the western coast of Africa for the majority of the fifteenth century, claiming exclusive rights for Portugal for its "lands of discoveries." Armed and enriched by imperial conquests in Asia, Africa, and the Americas, and the riches they provided in precious metals and trafficked human beings, Portugal became the first modern superpower and, for a time, the richest country in Europe.[9]

Two of these "discoveries" were what would become today's countries of Guinea-Bissau and Cape Verde. Explorers landed in Guinea-Bissau in 1446 and the nearby archipelago of Cape Verde in 1456. The former was then the center of the Mandinka kingdom of Kaabu, whose *mansa*s (rulers) exercised influence over broad swaths of western Africa with power gained from control over a hub of trans-Saharan trades of gold, ivory, and slaves.[10]

The captives from Kaabu's wars on the continent began to be sold into a new network of human trafficking that would far eclipse the network on the continent in size, scale, and depth of exploitation: the transatlantic slave trade, which funneled enslaved people and their labor into European colonial conquests.[11]

Most of these colonial territories, particularly in the initial centuries, were in the Americas. But Cape Verde was an exception. The chain of islands off Africa's western coast, un-inhabited and well suited as a stopover point in the emerging transoceanic trade, was then populated by Portuguese settlers and enslaved Africans. Cape Verde was also used as a staging point in the conquest of much of western Africa, including Guinea-Bissau, and Cape Verdeans were often afforded a middle managerial role in the both the slave trade and the colonial management of Guinea-Bissau.

By the time Lilica was born, well into the 1900s, European countries had used the wealth and power built up via the slave trade and their other global colonial efforts to establish formal colonial dominion over the vast majority of the African continent, including Cape Verde and Guinea-Bissau (then "Portuguese Guinea"). The Portuguese had long controlled their colonies with the callous indifference to suffering that was characteristic of the slave trade that the islands themselves enabled.

In response to one of the many droughts that plagued Cape Verde in the centuries leading up to its independence movement, colonial officials in London told a protesting Cape Verdean lawyer that "the government is not culpable that in Cabo Verde there have not been regular rains."[12] In all likelihood, Lilica's childhood was not so dissimilar from that of her parents or grandparents.

Portuguese militaries put down resistance to their rule with brutal military "pacification campaigns" to terrorize those who the famines and precarity did not silence.[13] This militarist posture was only intensified by the disintegration of the Portuguese democratic republic in 1926, which was replaced by a fascist regime installed under corporatist autocrat António Salazar called Estado Novo—the new state.[14]

In 1960, an organization rose to challenge the Estado Novo in Cape Verde and nearby Guinea-Bissau: the African Party for the Independence of Guinea and Cape Verde (PAIGC). The party spent three years negotiating with the Portuguese government, employing a strategy that focused on demonstrations and workers' strikes. The PAIGC's nonviolence was met with brutality, culminating in the massacre of fifty peacefully striking dockworkers at the port of Pidjiguiti.[15] After the massacre, the group began an armed guerrilla campaign of resistance to the Portuguese. This is the fight Lilica left school to join, and it culminated in the independence of both nations in 1973 and 1974.[16]

A number of factors contributed to the success of the PAIGC's multifaceted campaign, including the wave of African and Asian independence movements of the post–World War II decades (spearheaded by Ghana's independence in 1957) and the networks of mutual aid and solidarity that linked many of them, and particularly the African countries fighting against Portuguese domination (including Angola and Mozambique).

Historian Sónia Vaz Borges directs our attention toward an often-neglected aspect of their revolutionary activity: the PAIGC's militant education and consciousness raising practices.[17] Cape Verde and Guinea-Bissau inherited a colonial education system that was designed to produce and educate an elite class of "assimilated Africans" to comanage the colonial project and convert unassimilated "indigenous" Africans into a viable workforce.[18] By contrast, the militants of the PAIGC developed a program of education designed to counteract the ills of the Portuguese colonial education system and support self-determination and resistance to colonial rule.

The PAIGC's military struggle thus included a comprehensive battle on the "education front," which Bissau-Guinean militant Agnelo Regala said was considered "as important" as other fronts "because it is not worth . . . freeing the land if we are not ready to assume the responsibility of independence."[19] Basic literacy and political education were considered training for every aspect of the struggle.[20]

Through interviews with living PAIGC militants and archival research, Vaz Borges finds that they overcame a number of considerable practical hurdles. The PAIGC created and distributed a newspaper, even though low literacy rates among adults posed a challenge to its effectiveness. At the same time, schooling for children competed with their labor on the family farms and thus threatened the livelihood and survival of families who sustained themselves with subsistence farming. Partially as a result, the PAIGC's insistence on girls' inclusion in schools met with resistance in some parts of the countries. Security concerns and resource constraints, both exacerbated by the simultaneous armed struggle against the Portuguese military, always loomed large. Moreover, the PAIGC's secular education system threatened to interrupt a balance of power that had been carefully negotiated between the Portuguese, the Christian education system, and two other systems favored by the countries' Muslim and Animist communities.[21]

The PAIGC rose to meet these challenges through its cultivation of careful, strategic relationships, including with the newly formed Organization of African Unity, whose Liberation Committee served as a conduit for foreign material and military assistance to many of the anti-colonial movements on the continent, including from the Soviet Union and post-revolutionary China, which both donated substantial weapons and military training. Cuba, not content merely to contribute material assistance in the form of food and military uniforms, deployed troops—a step no other country took during the conflict.[22]

Ahmed Sékou Touré, president of the newly independent country of Guinea (neighboring Guinea-Bissau), donated a facility for a pilot boarding school. The party built the Escola Piloto with resources gained from the Red Cross and a high-ranking United Nations official (reputedly a "friend" to the liberation struggle). Lilica Boal was named the school's director.

Against this coalition was a parallel one lined up behind the Portuguese fascist state. Portugal, a NATO member, bombed Guinea-Bissau with the support of dozens of transport and bomber aircraft provided by Great Britain, France, Germany, the United States, and the American Lockheed corporation (now Lockheed Martin).[23]

The pilot school took in the children of PAIGC militants and the war orphans created by Portuguese bombs and infantry. There, Lilica and her comrades taught students, with considerable support from elsewhere in the world: they used materials printed in Sweden and funded partly by the Swedish Social Democratic Party, fed the children with provisions donated from Cuba (whose government also dispatched doctors to provide them health care), and maintained a laboratory for the students with resources from abroad.[24]

But, Vaz Borges explains, the PAIGC didn't stop at schools for children. They supplemented their adult and youth newspapers with collective reading and discussion circles, which especially facilitated adult education. To make children's education work, the party negotiated with village elders, working out a system in which children attended both PAIGC schools and religious schools, and integrated religious symbolism into party traditions.[25] They sent a contingent of women to the Soviet Union to receive education in nursing. After they returned, more girls enrolled. To facilitate the participation of children in a country of subsistence farmers, the school sessions were designed around the agricultural calendar.[26]

The full involvement of women in the liberation struggle was an explicit goal of the organization and was reflected in its organizing practices and regulations. For instance, the party eventually required that each of the elected village councils that helped organize the liberated zones include at least two women in its membership of five.[27] According to researcher Stephanie Urdang, from the time the first PAIGC mobilizers went to the countryside to hold consciousness-raising discussions in 1959, the party took only a decade to go from holding meetings that included just a handful of women to rough parity between men and women.[28] The armed wing of the party included a women's militia, which also produced many of the party's public health advisors.[29]

Cape Verde and Guinea-Bissau defeated the Portuguese Empire, winning national independence in 1973—an independence that was eventually recognized by the Portuguese government in 1975 after the previous year's revolution ousted the fascist Estado Novo regime.

The PAIGC went to work, transitioning from an armed struggle to one of a different kind: nation building. After seizing power in September 1973, the number of students in party programs more than doubled. But, having been focused on fighting the military, the party lacked the number of teachers needed for this new challenge. Nor did it have sufficient material resources to make new educational materials and quickly train cadres in the new educational method they had developed through the liberation struggle. As a result, Lilica Boal and her comrades felt their only option was to use existing colonial Portuguese educational materials and structures, but to "safely transform them."[30]

Paulo Freire and the Institute for Cultural Action (IDAC), of which he was a member and founder, were brought on to serve as advisors. This was in part because of the similarities in perspective between the framework for education the PAIGC had developed during the liberation struggle (aided by the pioneering contribution of the militants of the pilot school) and the theory Freire had elaborated before his exile from Brazil.[31]

Despite these efforts, there was no fairy-tale ending. The war with Portugal had destroyed much of Guinea-Bissau's infrastructure, cutting available arable land to less than a third of prewar levels—partially as a result of the Portuguese military's extensive bombing campaigns and herding of villagers who wouldn't (or couldn't) align with the PAIGC into small, dense farming plots that rapidly exhausted the soil.[32]

Economic crisis in Guinea-Bissau exacerbated social divisions: between the party and traditional leaders, between urban and rural parts of the countries, between different ethnic groups, and, perhaps most significantly, between Bissau-Guineans and Cape Verdeans. The Cape Verdeans, who were said to occupy a disproportionate number of leadership positions in the party, were often urban intellectuals whose participation had different stakes from the peasantry exposed to the worst of the war's violence and suffering, since nearly all of the early fighting of the war took place in Guinea-Bissau.[33] Moreover, the Cape Verdeans were likely deeply resented for the islands' long preferential treatment by the Portuguese Empire and middle managerial role in colonial domination.[34]

These tensions culminated in a 1980 coup that ousted the Cape Verdean wing of the party, which became the African Party for the Independence of Cape Verde (PAICV), remaining a major party in Cape Verdean politics to this day. Guinea-Bissau has been plagued by a pattern of coups and countercoups ever since, as different factions have fought for power in and around the party; in turn, power has become increasingly concentrated in the hands of party elites, including the ex-PAIGC militants.[35] Bissau-Guinean historian Julião Soares Sousa laments what he takes to be the products of the country's "painful recent history": the stigma brought by the fights for power and control, Guineans' lack of confidence in the political system and the party, the lack of effective action by the new elites in the face of the country's mounting problems, and, underlying all of the above, a deep-seated perversion of values.[36]

Making matters worse, increased policing of drug trafficking in Latin America made Guinea-Bissau a center of the global illicit drug trade, particularly of cocaine. Just as their location on Africa's western coast made Cape Verde and Guinea-Bissau strategic locations for the transatlantic slave trade, drug traffickers flocked to Guinea-Bissau as a stopover point between Venezuela and Colombia, and the lucrative European drug market. Global media christened Guinea-Bissau "Africa's first narco-state," estimating that as much as a quarter of the world's cocaine was trafficked through the small nation, though scholars tend to temper such claims.[37] Recent trends, including an "all-time high" of global cocaine consumption, have led some commentators to speculate that drug traffickers may be trying to expand trafficking both in and through Cape Verde in a similar fashion.[38]

Nevertheless, something meaningful was won, beyond new flags. Even Guinea-Bissau, regarded by many as a "failed state" (when not as a "narco-state"), has won some ground.[39] Education is one such arena: using its newfound national independence, Guinea-Bissau's literacy rate surged from its pre-independence level of 2 percent, climbing as high as 60 percent among fifteen- to twenty-four-year-olds.[40]

In the decades since independence, Cape Verde increased its national income tenfold, ascending from a status as one of the poorest countries in the world to a "middle-income country" and one of Africa's most stable economies.[41] The PAIGC's emphasis on community power and decision making seems to have survived, avoiding the temptations toward autocracy to which other revolutions succumbed, and some foreign commentators have gone as far as to call it an "African exception" and "Africa's most democratic nation."[42]

These revolutionary struggles did not just liberate Cape Verde and Guinea-Bissau—they also liberated Portugal. Lilica Boal recalls the insistence of Amílcar Cabral, one of the PAIGC's leaders, that their struggle was against colonialism as a system, not against the people of Portugal.[43] The party followed through on this commitment in deed as well: white militant Carmen Pereira was a high ranking political commissar and among the most prominent members of the party.[44] She explained her position on identity politics to journalist Suzanne Lipinska in simple terms that we should take to heart: "There are white people who oppress us and there are ones who help us."[45] In a radio address in 1969 aptly titled "Message to the People of Portugal," Cabral made this plain to the whole world, explicitly positioning the PAIGC as on the side of the Portuguese people against the Estado Novo government.[46]

While this was undoubtedly clever wartime propaganda, it was more than that. The PAIGC showed leniency to Portuguese prisoners of war, often releasing them—attempting to go beyond words and communicate in deed the difference between themselves and the Portuguese army, which often summarily executed PAIGC militants who had the misfortune of falling into enemy hands.[47] Cabral, like many of his and Lilica's comrades from Portugal's African colonies, was educated in Lisbon—there, he had been a leading member of antifascist groups, taking risky political action against the Estado Novo regime with Black comrades like Agostinho

Neto of Angola and white comrades like Mário Soares (future leader of the Portuguese Socialist Party and also future president of post–Estado Novo Portugal).[48] Ethnic Studies scholar Reiland Rabaka describes Cabral's thinking as "global and historical theory," with political aims and aspirations to match: Cabral recognized imperialism as the structure of the whole planet, not just of conditions in Cape Verde and Guinea-Bissau, and he thus recognized that countering imperialism required changing everyone's political structure and not just that of his own people's.[49]

But it would also prove to be more than a mere symbolic stance of solidarity with his comrades. The colonial wars in Guinea-Bissau, as well as in Angola and Mozambique, were steadily eroding support for the Estado Novo regime among capitalist and clergy elites alike.[50] Four years after Cabral's address, left-wing military officers met in secret to challenge the Estado Novo regime; many of them met and plotted in Guinea-Bissau, the theater of the anti-colonial battles where the Portuguese military forces were most seriously contemplating defeat.[51] These officers eventually formed the Armed Forces Movement (MFA) that toppled the Estado Novo regime after it failed to meet the movement's core demands of the "three *D*s": democracy, development, and decolonization.[52] Their largely bloodless (in Portugal, anyway) takeover is now known as the Carnation Revolution of 1974—so named because of the many images that circulated of ecstatic citizens handing soldiers carnations to celebrate the end of the fascist regime.[53] Though many underline the Carnation Revolution as a key turning point leading to decolonization, sociologist António Tomás points out that this idea is exactly backward: it was the revolutionary struggles of the PAIGC and their various comrades-in-arms that precipitated Portugal's partial decolonization, not the other way around.[54]

We've Got This

The PAIGC took on an important struggle against long odds, and their victories changed things for everyone. They could not erase or undo the barriers history had erected, but they could and did surpass many of them.

Chapters 2 and 3 painted a stark picture. Not only does social structure shape the environments in which we act with each other into worlds that serve elite interests, but it can subtly pervert our attempts to resist this elite domination. Some of the very actions we take to resist oppressive hierarchies end up serving them. Not exactly a hopeful turn.

But not all is lost. As we saw in the discussion of fable of the emperor's imaginary wardrobe, power structures affect even our most mundane interactions. But the conclusion of that story is equally consequential: a small child points and laughs at the emperor, failing to follow the rules or be intimidated. The spell of structural hierarchy is broken, and everyone can say aloud what they all were thinking: the emperor has no clothes!

There's a clear sense in which social structures organize our interactions: it builds the world in which they happen. This includes "affordances," usable aspects of the built social environment. If you want to make something easy to carry, give it a handle. If you want people to avoid having to walk on the road, pave a sidewalk and paint a crosswalk.

The world in which we act also includes incentives, the carrots and sticks that guide our behavior. In general, people are more likely to do things for which they're rewarded and less likely to do things for which they are punished.

There are limitations, of course. Social structures entail strong constraints that can render certain actions not just undesirable or unpopular, but literally impossible. One cannot "decolonize" the curriculum of a school that was not built in the first place. More darkly: a person cannot organize against your government if they have mysteriously fallen out of a helicopter or been imprisoned in a black site.

There are other strong and similarly effective forms of constraint: the terror inflicted on the loved ones of those thrown from helicopters, the physical presence of the surveilling overseer or manager. As Noam Chomsky put it in *Media Control:* "In what is nowadays called a totalitarian state, or a military state, it's easy. You just hold a bludgeon over their heads, and if they get out of line you smash them over the head."[55]

But these strongarm forms of restraint usually involve costly interventions. They require more attention and money, and invite more severe reprisals than elites tend to care to risk.

This is why most social structures rely on weaker enforcement mechanisms to police social life. They build affordances that herd people into the behavior that they would like, making it easy to do things that support the system and difficult to do things that do not. The upshot is that they maintain unbalanced and self-protective distributions of reward and punishment.

A classic way of doing this is to manipulate information through propaganda and disinformation. It's worth remembering that our information environment—our "systems of education," to use Carter G. Woodson's term—are less about strong-arm indoctrination of people and more about making system-preserving uses of information easy while rendering system-altering uses of information difficult.

Misinformation and propaganda often succeed at misleading, distracting, and misinforming. But they needn't. What's important politically is the result of such efforts in terms of what people do and don't do. There are reasons other than bad ideas, as we've already seen, that someone might compliment the emperor's robe or avoid making fun of him.

Some aspects of social policing are focused squarely on changing people's decisions without directly changing what they think. For instance, a wide range of activist groups, including the Debt Collective and the Movement for Black Lives, along with thinkers like Fantu Cheru and Jeffrey Williams, have long noticed the disciplinary function of student, medical, and credit card debt.[56] Cheru argues that external debts pressured postrevolutionary African governments into deals with the International Monetary Fund, while Williams shows how mounting student debt in the United States is itself a new "mode of pedagogy" that is driving students out of disruptive organizing and into docile compliance with the status quo.[57]

But there's also a clear sense in which all of this world building and policing *fails* to constrain us. Creatures like us have a special power. Despite all our social programming, we can just *do* things. We can, to some extent at will, ignore what social structures have told us to do. We can ignore the sidewalk and walk in the street; we can carry the bag with handles from its underside. We can do the thing that will be punished; we can ignore the potential reward, choose the smaller prize. Moreover, we can accept the rewards and the punishments without accepting the "lessons" they are meant to teach us about who and what is worthy.

It is this kind of action, off the beaten path, that the small child takes when they see the emperor. It is also what Carter G. Woodson did in response to white supremacy, what Lilica Boal and her PAIGC comrades did in the face of Portuguese colonialism, and what Paulo Freire did in response to the hierarchies of Brazilian racial capitalism and the geopolitics of the Cold War.

Immense structures and entrenched interests spend immense time, money, and effort convincing us either that we do not have this power or that we had better not use it. It is not hard to see why: it is the kind of power that can very quickly turn the talk of the town into the butt of its jokes.

This power is one of many that helps explain why our social systems are not fixed—even ones as complicated as our current global system of capitalism. As we already saw with the common ground, its structure is something we can and do change regularly. We can walk in the street, even when there are sidewalks; we can drive on the wrong side of the road; we can read sentences from right to left. As you can tell from these examples, we don't necessarily have much to gain from engaging in just any old deviation from the social script. But with some effort and thoughtfulness, this is a power we can wield more constructively: We can decide to share information the boss tells us is sacrosanct. We can walk in the street to block traffic for the protest. And we can invite people to do these things with us.

Our capacity to make the systems we live in more complex, even while embedded in a world that structures our actions, is itself part of the system's overall *self-organization*, as environmental scientist and systems theorist Donella Meadows explains. Meadows notes a role for education that is strikingly similar to the one Woodson envisaged nearly a century earlier: "[C]onditions that encourage self-organization often can be scary for individuals and threatening to power structures. As a consequence, education systems may restrict the creative powers of children instead of stimulating those powers."[58]

Human social systems are self-organizing. Indeed, something much like this thought is already embedded in the use of the term "organizing" to label work that challenges oppressive aspects of our society. Often when we organize, we try to build a smaller system of our own within the overall system we live in that is influential enough to change the whole system's behavior. This is a potential role for a mass movement, a workers' party, a set of direct actions. It's the sort of thing we can do in a room.

In both Cape Verde and Guinea-Bissau, the PAIGC ran into obstacles to achieving a deeper freedom, beyond having a flag and ministers. This included internal dynamics, social cleavages that they could manage but not erase. But they also included external problems beyond the immediate control of their interpersonal dynamics and institutional choices, including resource constraints and the global drug trade.

In our organizing, there are two basic ways we can respond to this unfortunate fact about political struggle. The first is to shift our aims and priorities to focus on that which we can easily reach, either by ignoring the external constraints or simply by taking on faith that getting the "internal" politics right is our best shot of changing the world at large. While there is a wisdom to focusing on what we have the best chance of controlling or managing, this approach is also deeply defeatist. That's why, in any sober analysis of our situation, most of the tools we have to affect to change the world are part of a second, "external" strategy: one that lies outside of any given room or set of interpersonal relationships.

Getting Out the Hammers

If we follow the constructive approach that I am advocating in these pages, we recognize that the way we treat each other in organizing spaces matters primarily in terms of how it relates us to the rest of the world. After all, most of the world—and thus most of the structures we are trying to change—are outside of the particular rooms in which we build alliances and refine our politics.

Whatever the PAIGC got wrong, they got this right: both the militant education of the liberation struggle and the postrevolutionary construction of an education system were part and parcel of the same effort: one to change not just the dynamics of the classroom, but those of a whole society. They aimed to literally redraw the map of the world and change its power relations, and they tried to build the kinds of rooms that would support that outcome.

The water-contamination crisis in Flint, Michigan, presents another, more recent example of both the possibilities and limitations of refining our politics in this way. Michigan's Department of Environmental Quality (MDEQ), a government body tasked with the support of "healthy communities," with a team of fifty trained scientists at its disposal, was complicit in covering up the scale and gravity of the public health crisis for months after the 2014 switch of the city's water source to the heavily polluted Flint River.

After the American Civil Liberties Union circulated a leaked internal memo from the federal Environmental Protection Agency that expressed concern about lead in Flint water, the MDEQ produced a doctored report, putting the overall measure of lead levels within federally mandated levels by failing to count two contaminated samples. The MDEQ, speaking from a position of expertise and political authority, defended the status quo in Flint, claiming that "Flint water is safe to drink," which Flint mayor Dayne Walling cited in his statement aiming to "dispel myths and promote the truth about the Flint River."[59]

The month after the ill-fated switch in Flint's water source, residents reported that their tap water was discolored and gave off an alarming odor. In that moment, what they needed was not for their oppression to be "celebrated," "centered," or narrated in the newest academic parlance. They didn't need outsiders to empathize over what it felt like to be poisoned. To be sure, deference politics could give people these things—and these things aren't unimportant. But they are secondary. What Flint residents really needed, above all, was to get the lead out of their water.

So they got to work. The first step was to develop epistemic authority. To achieve this, they built a new room, one that put Flint residents and activists in active collaboration with scientists who had the laboratories to run the relevant tests and prove MDEQ's report was fraudulent.

Flint residents' outcry about the poisonings helped recruit scientists to their cause. The new roommates ran a citizen science campaign, further raising the alarm about the water quality and distributing sampling kits to neighbors so that they could submit their water for testing. The alliance of residents and scientists won, and the poisoning of the children of Flint emerged as a national scandal.

This victory over the public narrative was only a first step, however. The second step—cleaning the water—required more than state acknowledgment; it entailed the apportionment of labor and resources to fix the water and address continuing health concerns.

What Flint residents received, initially, was a mix of platitudes and mockery from the ruling elite (including the US president, whose shared racial identity with many of the Flint residents apparently did not constrain). Now, however, it looks as though the activism of Flint residents and their expanding list of coalition partners has won additional and more meaningful victories. As of this writing, the ongoing campaign is pushing the project to replace dangerous water service lines to its final stage and has already forced the State of Michigan to pay a $600 million settlement to affected families.

This outcome is in no way a wholesale victory. Not only will attorney fees cut a substantial portion from the payouts, but the settlement cannot undo the damage that was caused to the residents.

Indeed, no epistemic orientation can by itself undo the various power asymmetries between the people and the imperial state system. But constructive politics, like that of Flint's residents *can* help make the game a little more competitive; deference epistemology, on the other hand, isn't even playing.

Building a New House

At the end of the day, there's only so much we can accomplish in the room—in our organization, on our block, in our academic department, in our party. Getting the dynamics of our movements, communities, friend groups, and social networks right is important, but there's also the crucial question of how that internal work relates to other struggles.

Racial capitalism is itself a global system, and the pace and direction of the climate crisis it has wrought will be set by our successes and failures at that same planetary scale.[60]

At bottom, the constructive approach responds to this problem in a very simple fashion. Whether on a small scale or in a large institution, our orienting political goal is to *build things*, whether institutions, norms, or other tools. As we've just seen, the residents of Flint built a citizen-science structure to challenge the MDEQ. This is not a one-off story, but a generalizable strategy: even public decision-making that involves technical concepts and research can be done in a meaningfully democratic and participatory fashion.[61]

Like standpoint epistemology, this simple ethos seems obvious and innocuous enough at this level of abstraction. But it has competitors. For instance, people and organizations could orient their politics oppositionally. Many forms of political identification consist in whole or in large part as lists of things that one opposes: one is "anti-capitalist," "anti-carceral," or "antiracist." Racism, capitalism, and mass incarceration are worth opposing. But the long view of human history confirms that even successful opposition to these would not guarantee a just future. Not one of these phenomena, at least in their modern forms, is even a millennium old. Especially in recent history, more often than not, one form of oppression has been replaced with another, different form that is similar to or even more unjust than the one that preceded it.

But maybe we want more than to play Whac-A-Mole with injustice. If we want to do more than alter the color of our children's chains, we will have to successfully oppose more than isolated instances of oppression. I suspect that this is why prison scholar Ruth Wilson Gilmore stressed that "abolition is about presence, not absence" and fellow abolitionist Micah Herskind called it "the dual-pronged project of tearing down and building up, the dismantling of life-sucking systems alongside the construction of life-giving ones."[62] Gilmore and Herskind also strike a similar chord with the anti-colonial ethos of PAIGC militant Amílcar Cabral, which, in the words of Kenyan activist Firoze Manji, can be summarized as "self-determination, not secession."[63]

A constructive approach to politics involves building power in and through institutions and networks. Some of these operate apart from or in the margins of the more dominant global institutions: like the collective informal economic and mutual aid practices that Black peoples and others have practiced continuously over the past centuries.[64] But many needed institutions are well known, tried-and-true engines of social progress. Labor unions allow workers to bargain collectively over their working conditions and compensation—pivotal struggles in and of themselves that decide the basic economic and social conditions of life for scores of people. But the political potential of unions is, of course, even more significant than this. Organized workers can use their leverage for goals far beyond wages and benefits, and historically have often done so.

In the United States, unions played a pivotal role in dismantling the Jim Crow system of formal segregation and developing the concept and practice of a "just transition" of workers out of environmentally and socially harmful industries into beneficial ones.[65] Correspondingly, it was a courageous strike by workers (and its violent repression by colonial police) that launched the PAIGC's successful anti-colonial struggle.[66] More recently, Egyptian, Algerian, and Kuwaiti trade unions have defied bans and repression to force concessions from the regimes whose abuses sparked the Arab Spring uprisings of 2011, as well as from the ones that followed it.[67]

Some of the other institutions we will have to build may be less familiar. In 2013, a coalition of organizers launched a crowd-funded "Rolling Jubilee" campaign to erase more than $30 million worth of medical, tuition, payday loan, and criminal debt for thousands of unaffiliated people. That coalition morphed into a debtors' union called the Debt Collective.

Student debt alone in the United States is worth $1.7 trillion—which, the Debt Collective points out, turns into $1.7 trillion worth of leverage on the global financial system if it is tightly organized.

Around the world, organizations fighting for housing justice, ranging from squatters' groups to tenants' unions, are challenging the dictates of capital over housing markets.[68] As the Debt Collective point outs, these old and new formations can be mutually supporting partners. An illustrative example is the successful revolt of the people of Cochabamba, Bolivia, against the privatization of the city's water system by US-based multinational Bechtel—a movement that employed a combination of general strikes and guerilla military tactics to preserve public control over the commons.[69]

But a constructive approach to politics calls for us to build power expansively, across all aspects of social life—beyond just work. This is especially important in the digital era. Among the threats posed by this most recent stage of racial capitalism are the erosion of the practical and material bases for popular power over knowledge production and distribution.

The capture and corruption of these bases by well-positioned elites, especially tech corporations, goes on unabated and largely unchallenged.

We are seeing the corporate monopolization of local news and social media, the ongoing destruction and looting of the journalistic profession, and the domination of elite interests in the production of knowledge by research universities and think tanks. But, as the long history of muckraking, abolitionist newspapers, consciousness raising, and political education campaigns shows, information networks aid effective political action and can constrain the system's violence. Many people are hard at work developing their twenty-first-century analogues, building strong networks for movement journalism, encouraging adoption of alternative social media platforms, and increasing the research capacity of left organizations. They deserve and need our support.

Rules and procedures can help keep these ventures stable and well directed. But *Robert's Rules of Order* cannot do much to constrain toxic organizing cultures. We will have to think more comprehensively.

In a speech describing social movements like the anti-imperialist struggles he was then fighting against the Portuguese Empire, Cabral observed that "national liberation is necessarily an act of culture."[70] By "culture," Cabral did not mean that a carefully curated list of customary greetings, traditional foods, and styles of dress were themselves going to bring down the military forces of a fascist empire.

Culture is "the vigorous manifestation on the ideological or idealist plane" of people and "a product of their history,"

Cabral observed. But he also insisted that culture is not just an idle ideological force or set of fashions and preferences that results from past and present trends; it is also "a determinant of history, by the positive or negative influence which it exerts on the evolution of relationships between man and his environment." This is why he claimed that imperialist domination "can be maintained only by the permanent, organized repression of the cultural life of the people concerned." After all, if people are in the habit of determining for themselves how to organize more of their lives than they are currently allowed to, cunning imperialists understand that the colonized might eventually go for the whole pie. In this sense, then, the struggle for national liberation was simply "the organized political expression of the culture of the people who are undertaking the struggle."[71] We should put our cultural norms to the same constructive test as our other goals and aspirations: "The important thing is to proceed to critical analysis of African cultures in relation to the liberation movement and to the exigencies of progress." That is, we should evaluate our culture instrumentally, by how well it helps us build what we are trying to build.[72]

A constructive political culture would focus on outcome over process—the pursuit of specific goals or end results rather than avoiding complicity in injustice or promoting purely moral or aesthetic principles.

When it comes to knowledge and information, we should be concerned primarily with building institutions and campaign-relevant practices of information gathering and sharing rather than centering specific groups of people or spokespeople who stand in for them. And we should calibrate our program directly to the task of redistributing social resources and power rather than to pedestals, attention, or symbolism.

We need to focus on building and rebuilding rooms, not on regulating traffic within and between them. This is a world-making project aimed at building and rebuilding actual structures of social connection and movement, not mere critique of the ones we already have.

We should set our sights on different scales, from local fights like community control over land, housing, and energy to global ones over debt cancellation in the global South. These fights, especially when they are planetary in scope, make it possible to totally revamp our global social system—to rebuild the house we all live in together.

5

The Point
Is to Change It

Writing in the 1880s, Karl Marx famously observed, "Philosophers have only interpreted the world, in various ways; the point, however, is to change it."[1] After all, no matter who we "center" in our organizing culture's thoughts and messages, there will be lead in our water until and unless we do something about the pipes.

Over a century later and an ocean away, Afro-Guyanese activist and intellectual Andaiye sounded a similar alarm: "Old foundations are crumbling," she warned, "and new ones are not yet being imagined."

I'm not alone in seeing an affinity between these lines of thinking: it was for good reason that Alissa Trotz, editor of the collection of Andaiye's essays in which I discovered this quote, gave the book the title *The Point Is to Change the World* and included Marx's eleventh thesis on Feuerbach as its epigraph.[2]

But while Marx's comment encapsulates the ancient struggle over the place of philosophy in any age, Andaiye's

114

provokes us to examine its relevance in this one.

Andaiye was born on September 11, 1941, in George-town, the capital of what was then British Guiana. With the approval of President John F. Kennedy, the CIA conspired to rig the soon-to-be-independent country's elections, ousting the outspokenly Communist Indo-Guyanese Cheddi Jagan in favor of a perceived moderate, Forbes Burnham. His rule, which Guyanese historian Clem Seecharan characterizes as a dictatorship, would last for sixteen years.[3]

While her country descended into what Seecharan describes as a "virtual racial war between Africans and Indians," a young Andaiye was hard at work educating herself and deepening her radical politics. She studied at the University of the West Indies with fellow student and eventual comrade Walter Rodney, and later lectured in a program for "disadvantaged students" in the United States. She returned home with a staunch feminist and Marxist politics rooted in solidarity. Among her many Guya-nese organizational affiliations were the Red Thread women's organization and the Working People's Alliance.

By 2009, when she was invited to give a commencement speech at her alma mater, Andaiye was a veteran activist, deeply attuned to the stakes of political analysis. And when she observed that "old foundations are crumbling, and new ones are not yet being imagined," she was not talking about the structure of philosophical analysis or patterns of political discourse. She was talking about the weather.

Andaiye went on to explain that "old assumptions about weather patterns and how these shape major economic occu-pations are no longer valid."[4] Climate crises in the Caribbean were mounting. At the time, climate change might have seemed like a drop in the bucket in larger countries with advanced economies, but for the small island states of the Caribbean, it already posed an existential crisis. In 2005, her home country lost the equivalent of 60 percent of its gross domestic product in a single flood that covered a mere twenty-five miles of its more than two hundred–mile coastline.[5]

Such ecological crises are exacerbating long-standing forms of injustice in the world economy. For instance, after the flooding in Guyana, women caregivers and subsistence farmers shouldered massively increased burdens.

The North American Free Trade Agreement (NAFTA) likewise contributed to gender injustices. Women were shuffled out of sectors like manufacturing at rates more than double those of men, increasing their already-disproportionate representation in the precarious informal sector. Massive majorities of farming populations in Dominica were shunted out of the relatively secure formal sector into the informal sector. Racial violence increased in Guyana, police violence spiked in Jamaica, and domestic and sexual violence surged throughout the region.

Confronted by these crises, Andaiye said, such countries turned where they had to for funds: the International Monetary Fund. And they did so despite the fact that little had changed since the financial institution's disastrous structural adjustment policies of the 1970s.

In response, Andaiye called for imagination—not to more incisively describe the failures of the first or second wave of policies, but to overcome the lack of new solutions that forced the region back to familiar and available nonsolutions. She called for builders.

Andaiye was in good company. Abolitionist scholar Ruth Wilson Gilmore, in her classic book *Golden Gulag*, documents a deep irony of the rise of California's prison system, especially given US capitalism's long-standing anti-communism: its world historical levels of incarceration were built via tight coordination between corporations, bankers, and government officials—that is, "central planning." But Gilmore also noticed something about the successful resistance of California communities, including one in Tulane County, where family ranchers and farmworkers united under the banners of the United Farm Workers fought off a planned prison construction. Even without the "technocratic expertise" that the bankers and state government wielded, the community's activists put forward "alternate planning criteria that must precede any industrial location decision," which Gilmore calls "grassroots planning."[6]

Both Andaiye and Gilmore propose, then, that planning creates places. The question the constructive program asks is: Will the plans be theirs or ours?

What the Constructive Approach Asks of Us

The constructive approach to politics does not ask us to invent a political culture out of whole cloth. "Constructive" is just a name, after all. Many of the people who came before us, including those profiled in this book, practiced constructive politics without having any need of this particular word to describe what they were doing.

A constructive program does not ask us to ignore our own interpersonal, symbolic, or material needs, even though it does ask us to be disciplined in how we relate those to the needs of the struggle and of the scores of people and generations that are not immediately present. After reading the book *Woman Power* by Cellestine Ware, Demita Frazier of the Combahee River Collective recalls arriving at the view that it is both Black women's "right and responsibility" to analyze their social position as part of their radical perspective.[7] I think the rest of us should take a page from this book as well.

The constructive approach is, however, extremely demanding. It asks us to be planners and designers, to be accountable and responsive to people who aren't yet in the room. In addition to being architects, it asks us to become builders and construction workers: to actually build the kinds of rooms we could sit in together, rather than idly speculate about which rooms would be nice. But it's important to acknowledge, in closing this book, that the constructive approach has implicit moral and emotional demands, as well: we can neither plan nor build a better world without collectively cultivating diverse kinds of moral and emotional discipline.

The deferential approach to politics is worth praising because of its concern and attention to the importance of lived experience—especially traumatic experiences. But just as this virtue becomes a vice when "being in the room" effects are ignored, this virtue also becomes a vice when trauma's importance and prevalence are framed as positive bases for social credentials and deference behaviors, rather than primarily as problems to deal with collectively.

Here, scholarly analysis and argument fail me. The remainder of what I have to say skews more toward conviction than contention. But life has taught me that conviction has much to teach, however differently posed or processed, and so I press on.

I take concerns about trauma especially seriously. I grew up in the United States, a nation structured by settler colonialism, racial slavery, and their aftermath, with enough collective and historical trauma to go around. I also grew up in a Nigerian diasporic community, populated by many who had genocide in their living memory.

At the national and community level, I have seen personality traits, quirks of habit and action, that I've suspected were born of these grim parts of history. Like most people, I have not been spared. I've watched and felt myself change in reaction to fearing for my dignity or life, to crushing pain and humiliation. I reflect on these traumatic moments often, and very seldom do I think, "That was educational."

These experiences can be, if we are very fortunate, building blocks. What comes of them depends on how the blocks are put together. Those who study the politics of knowledge call this the "achievement thesis." As philosopher Briana Toole clarifies, by itself, one's social location only puts a person in a position to know; "epistemic privilege" or advantage, on the other hand, is achieved only through deliberate, concerted struggle from that position.[8]

Humiliation, deprivation, and suffering can build—especially in the context of the deliberate, structured effort of "consciousness raising" that Toole specifically highlights. But these same experiences can also destroy, and if I had to bet on which effect would win most often, it would be the latter.

Contra the old expression, pain, whether born of oppression or not, is a poor teacher. Suffering is partial, shortsighted, and self-absorbed. We shouldn't have a politics that expects different. Oppression is not a prep school.

Demanding as the constructive approach may be, the deferential approach is far more so, and in a far more unfair way. As philosopher Agnes Callard rightly notes, trauma (and even the righteous, well-deserved anger that often accompanies it) can corrupt as readily as it can ennoble.[9] Perhaps more so.

When it comes down to it, the thing I believe most deeply about deference politics is that it asks something of trauma that it cannot give. It asks the traumatized to shoulder burdens alone that we ought to share collectively, lifting them up onto a pedestal in order to hide below them.

When I think about my trauma, I don't think about life lessons. I think about the quiet nobility of survival. The very fact that those chapters weren't the final ones of my story is powerful enough all on its own. It is enough to ask of those experiences that I am still here to remember them.

I also believe that deference politics asks us to be less than we are—and not even for our own benefit. As scholar-activist Nick Estes explains in the context of Indigenous politics, "The cunning of trauma politics is that it turns actual people and struggles, whether racial or Indigenous citizenship and belonging, into matters of injury. It defines an entire people mostly on their trauma and not by their aspirations or sheer humanity." This performance is not for the benefit of Indigenous people; rather, "it's for white audiences or institutions of power."[10]

When I think about my trauma, I also think about the great writer James Baldwin's realization that the things that most tormented him "were the very things that connected me with all the people who were alive, or who had ever been alive."[11]

That I have experienced my share of traumatic experiences, have survived abuse of various kinds, have faced near death from accidental circumstance and from violence (different as the particulars of these may be from those around me) is not a card to play in gamified social interaction or a weapon to wield in battles over prestige. It is not what gives me a special right to speak, to evaluate, or to decide for a group. It is a concrete, experiential manifestation of the vulnerability that connects me to most of the people on this earth. It comes between me and other people not as a wall, but as a bridge.

Going together—the politics of solidarity, which deference provides one, flawed model of doing—is a good start. But on its own, it's not enough. We also have to decide collectively where we're going, and then we have to do what it takes to get there. Though we start from different levels of privilege or advantage, this journey is not a matter of figuring out who should bow to whom, but simply one of figuring out how best to join forces. As Paulo Freire showed us in theory, and the African anti-colonial and Portuguese Carnation revolutions showed us in practice, we will need each other to get where we're going. And getting there, after all, is the point.

Notes

Introduction

An earlier version of this essay appeared as "Identity Politics and Elite Capture," *Boston Review*, May 7, 2020, https://bostonreview.net/articles/olufemi-o-taiwo-identity-politics-and-elite-capture/.

1. Amílcar Cabral, *Unity and Struggle: Speeches and Writings of Amílcar Cabral*, vol. 3 (New York: New York University Press, 1979), 86.

2. Max Bearak and Rael Ombuor, "Kenyan Police Shot Dead a Teenager on His Balcony during a Coronavirus Curfew Crackdown," *Washington Post*, March 31, 2021, https://www .washingtonpost.com/world/africa/kenyan-police-shot-dead -a-teenager-on-his-balcony-during-a-coronavirus-curfew -crackdown/2020/03/31/6344c70e-7350-11ea-ad9b -254ec99993bc_story.html.

3. Jorge Valencia, "Black Lives Matter Protests Renew Parallel Debates in Brazil, Colombia," *The World*, June 15, 2021, https://www.pri.org/stories/2020-06-15/black-lives -matter-protests-renew-parallel-debates-brazil-colombia.

4. "Demonstrators in Brazil Protest against Crimes Committed by Police," *VOA News*, June 1, 2020, https:// www.voanews.com/americas/demonstrators-brazil -protest-against-crimes-committed-police.

5. César Muñoz, "Brazil Suffers Its Own Scourge of Police Brutality," *Human Rights Watch*, June 3, 2020, https://www

.hrw.org/news/2020/06/03/brazil-suffers-its-own-scourge
-police-brutality.

6. "Rio Violence: Police Killings Reach Record High in 2019,"
BBC News, January 23, 2020, https://www.bbc.com/news
/world-latin-america-51220364.

7. Larry Buchanan, Quoctrung Bui, and Jugal K. Patel, "Black
Lives Matter May Be the Largest Movement in U.S. History,"
New York Times, July 3, 2020, https://www.nytimes.com
/interactive/2020/07/03/us/george-floyd-protests-crowd-size
.html; Dudley L. Preston, "3 Ways That the U.S. Population
Will Change over the Next Decade," *PBS NewsHour*, accessed
January 2, 2020, https://www.pbs.org/newshour/nation
/3-ways-that-the-u-s-population-will-change-over-the
-next-decade.

8. Jen Kirby, "'Black Lives Matter' Has Become a Global Rally-
ing Cry," *Vox*, June 12, 2020, https://www.vox.com
/2020/6/12/21285244/black-lives-matter-global-protests
-george-floyd-uk-belgium.

9. "Nigeria's Lekki Shooting: What Has Happened so Far at
Lagos Judicial Panel," *BBC News*, November 27, 2020,
https://www.bbc.com/news/world-africa-55099016.

10. I explore this question in greater depth in my book *Reconsid-
ering Reparations: Worldmaking in the Case of Climate Crisis*
(New York: Oxford University Press, 2021); Kwame Nkrumah,
"Neo-Colonialism: The Last Stage of Imperialism," 1967; F
Pigeaud and NS Sylla, "Africa's Last Colonial Currency: The
CFA Franc Story," 2021.

11. David Malpass, "June 18, 2020: Ending Racism," *Voices*, June
18, 2020, https://blogs.worldbank.org/voices/june-18-2020
-ending-racism; Chris Cannito, "UN Human Rights Council
Holds Historic Hearings on Racism in US," *Nonprofit Quarterly*, June 22, 2020, https://nonprofitquarterly.org/un-human
-rights-council-holds-historic-hearings-on-racism-in-us/.

12. Roberto Lovato, "The Age of Intersectional Empire Is Upon Us," May 10, 2021, *The Nation*, https://www.thenation.com/article/politics/cia-video-intersectional/.

13. Talia Lavin, "The 1960s Previewed the GOP Attack on 'Critical Race Theory,'" *MSNBC*, June 22, 2021, https://www.msnbc.com/opinion/right-wing-freakout-about-critical-race-theory-began-1960s-n1271670; Kevin M. Kruse, "The Trump Administration's Thinly-Veiled Rebuke of 'The 1619 Project' is a Sloppy, Racist Mess," *MSNBC*, accessed January 20, 2021, https://www.msnbc.com/opinion/trump-administration-s-thinly-veiled-rebuke-1619-project-sloppy-racist-n1254807.

14. Amy Cassidy and Tara John, "UN Condemns 'Reprehensible' UK Race Report for Repackaging 'Racist Tropes into Fact,'" *CNN*, April 19, 2021, https://www.cnn.com/2021/04/19/uk/un-uk-race-report-intl-gbr/index.html; Tara John, "Analysis: Culture Wars Give Boris Johnson and His Government a Quick and Easy High. They're No Substitute for Governing," *CNN*, accessed April 4, 2021, https://www.cnn.com/2021/04/04/uk/uk-race-report-culture-wars-intl-gbr/index.html.

15. Ashley Bohrer, "Intersectionality and Marxism: A Critical Historiography," *Historical Materialism* 26, no. 2 (2018): 60.

16. Dominic Gustavo, "'Humans of CIA' Recruitment Campaign Sells Youth 'Identity Politics Imperialism,'" *World Socialist Web Site*, May 20, 2021, https://www.wsws.org/en/articles/2021/05/20/ciar-m20.html.

17. Duchess Harris, "From the Kennedy Commission to the Combahee Collective," in *Sisters in the Struggle* (New York: New York University Press, 2001), 280–305.

18. Harris, "Combahee Collective," 280–305.

19. Keeanga-Yamahtta Taylor, *How We Get Free: Black Feminism and the Combahee River Collective* (Chicago: Haymarket Books, 2017), 5–6 (my emphasis).

20. Terrell Jermaine Starr, "Barbara Smith, Who Helped Coin the Term 'Identity Politics,' Endorses Bernie Sanders," *The Root*, accessed February 3, 2020, https://www.theroot.com/barbara -smith-who-helped-coin-the-term-identity-politi-1841419291; Barbara Smith, "I Helped Coin the Term 'Identity Politics'. I'm Endorsing Bernie Sanders," *Guardian*, February 10, 2020, http://www.theguardian.com/commentisfree/2020/feb/10 /identity-politics-bernie-sanders-endorsement.

21. Taylor, *How We Get Free*, 107–9.

22. Starr, "Barbara Smith Endorses Bernie Sanders."

23. Asad Haider, "Identity Politics," chapter 1 in *Mistaken Identity: Race and Class in the Age of Trump* (Verso Books, 2018), 7–26.

24. Marie Moran, "(Un) Troubling Identity Politics: A Cultural Materialist Intervention," *European Journal of Social Theory* 23, no. 2 (2020): 258–77; Linda Martín Alcoff, "The Political Critique," chapter 2 in *Visible Identities: Race, Gender, and the Self* (Oxford University Press, 2005), 20–46.

25. Tess Bonn, "Saagar Enjeti Laments Use of Identity Politics in 2020 Democratic Race," *The Hill*, November 26, 2019, https:// thehill.com/hilltv/rising/472191-saagar-enjeti-laments-use -of-identity-politics-in-2020-democratic-race.

26. Michael C. Dawson, *Blacks in and out of the Left* (Cambridge, MA: Harvard University Press, 2013), 194.

27. Adom Getachew, *Worldmaking after Empire: The Rise and Fall of Self-Determination* (Princeton, NJ: Princeton University Press, 2019).

Chapter 1: What Is Elite Capture?

1. Tony Platt, "E. Franklin Frazier Reconsidered," *Social Justice* 16, no. 4 (1989): 186–95; Malik Simba, "E. Franklin Frazier (1894– 1962)," *Black Past*, January 19, 2007, https://www.blackpast.org

/african-american-history/frazier-e-franklin-1894-1962/; Arthur P. Davis, "E. Franklin Frazier (1894–1962): A Profile," *Journal of Negro Education* 31, no. 4 (1962): 429–35.

2. Tony Platt and Susan Chandler, "Constant Struggle: E. Franklin Frazier and Black Social Work in the 1920s," *Social Work* 33, no. 4 (1988): 293–97.

3. Frazier's 1939 book *The Negro Family in the United States* was a widely acclaimed sociological account of Black American life. See Randal Maurice Jelks and Ayesha K. Hardison, "Black Love after E. Franklin Frazier: An Introduction," *Women, Gender, and Families of Color* 7, no. 2 (2019): 108–12.

4. Lori Martin, "Africana Demography: Lessons from Founders E. Franklin Frazier, WEB Du Bois, and the Atlanta School of Sociology," *Issues in Race and Society* 8 (2019): 5–28; Earl Wright and Thomas C. Calhoun, "Jim Crow Sociology: Toward an Understanding of the Origin and Principles of Black Sociology via the Atlanta Sociological Laboratory," *Sociological Focus* 39, no. 1 (2006): 1–18.

5. Frantz Fanon, *The Wretched of the Earth*, Constance Farrington, trans. (New York: Grove, 1963), 149–51.

6. Fanon, *Wretched of the Earth*, 148.

7. Fanon, "The Trials and Tribulations of National Consciousness," chapter 3 in *The Wretched of the Earth* (1961), Richard Philcox, trans. (New York: Grove, 2004), 97–144.

8. Kwame Nkrumah, *Neo-Colonialism: The Last Stage of Imperialism* (New York: International Publishers, 1966).

9. Bernard Magubane and Nzongola-Ntalaja, *Proletarianization and Class Struggle in Africa* (San Francisco: Synthesis Publications, n.d.), 57.

10. Fanon, *Wretched of the Earth* (2004 ed.), 97–144.

11. E. Franklin Frazier, *Black Bourgeoisie* (New York: Free Press, 1997), 104.

12. Frazier, "Negro Business: A Social Myth," chapter 7 in *Black*

Bourgeoisie, 153–73.

13. Frazier, *Black Bourgeoisie*, 235.

14. Frazier, *Black Bourgeoisie*, 236.

15. Jared A. Ball, *The Myth and Propaganda of Black Buying Power* (New York: Springer, 2020).

16. Ball, "Introduction" in *Black Buying Power*, 1–10.

17. Jo Freeman, "The Tyranny of Stucturelessness," Jo Freeman official website, https://www.jofreeman.com/joreen/tyranny.htm.

18. For examples, see Monica Martinez-Bravo, Priya Mukherjee, and Andreas Stegmann, "The Non-democratic Roots of Elite Capture: Evidence from Soeharto Mayors in Indonesia," *Econometrica* 85, no. 6 (2017): 1991–2010; Pranab K. Bardhan and Dilip Mookherjee, "Capture and Governance at Local and National Levels," *American Economic Review* 90, no. 2 (2000): 135–39; Daron Acemoglu and James A. Robinson, "Persistence of Power, Elites, and Institutions," *American Economic Review* 98, no. 1 (2008): 267–93.

19. Diya Dutta, "Elite Capture and Corruption: Concepts and Definitions," *National Council of Applied Economic Research*, 2009, 4.

20. Dutta, "Elite Capture and Corruption," 5.

21. Wendy Brown, "Neo-Liberalism and the End of Liberal Democracy," *Theory and Event* 7, no. 1 (2003); Tyler Stovall, *White Freedom: The Racial History of an Idea* (Princeton, NJ: Princeton University Press, 2021).

22. Keeanga-Yamahtta Taylor, *From#BlackLivesMatter to Black Liberation* (Chicago: Haymarket Books, 2016), 100.

23. Cited in David Farber, *Crack: Rock Cocaine, Street Capitalism, and the Decade of Greed* (Cambridge, UK: Cambridge University Press, 2019), 144.

24. Ryan Devereaux, "How the CIA Watched Over the Destruction of Gary Webb," *The Intercept*, September 25, 2014, https://theintercept.com/2014/09/25/managing-nightmare -cia-media-destruction-gary-webb/.

25. Neil Fligstein and Linda Markowitz, "Financial Reorganization of American Corporations in the 1980s," *Sociology and the Public Agenda*, 1993, 185–206; Neil Fligstein and Taek-Jin Shin, "The Shareholder Value Society: A Review of the Changes in Working Conditions and Inequality in the United States, 1976 to 2000," *Social Inequality*, 2004, 401–32; Samuel Knafo and Sahil Jai Dutta, "The Myth of the Shareholder Revolution and the Financialization of the Firm," *Review of International Political Economy* 27, no. 3 (2020): 476–99; Peter Nolan, Jin Zhang, and Chunhang Liu, "The Global Business Revolution, the Cascade Effect, and the Challenge for Firms from Developing Countries," *Cambridge Journal of Economics* 32, no. 1 (2008): 42–43.

26. Doug Henwood, "Take Me to Your Leader: The Rot of the American Ruling Class," *Jacobin*, April 27, 2021, https://jacobinmag.com/2021/04/take-me-to-your-leader-the-rot-of-the-american-ruling-class.

27. Knafo and Dutta argue, alongside an earlier analysis by Fligstein and against much of the existing literature, that the 80s shareholder revolution was one phase in a longer arc of major changes in corporate governance. The quote in this section is from Nolan, Zhang, and Liu's analysis. Knafo and Dutta, "The Myth of the Shareholder Revolution and the Financialization of the Firm"; Nolan, Zhang, and Liu, "The Global Business Revolution, the Cascade Effect, and the Challenge for Firms from Developing Countries," 43.

28. Benjamin P. Edwards, "Arbitration's Dark Shadow," *Nev. LJ* 18 (2017): 427.

29. Daniela Gabor and Ndongo Samba Sylla, "Planting Budgetary Time Bombs in Africa: The Macron Doctrine En Marche," CADTM, September 18, 2021, https://www.cadtm.org/Planting-budgetary-time-bombs-in-Africa-the-Macron-Doctrine-En-Marche.

30. Karen Hao, "Troll Farms Reached 140 Million Americans a

Month on Facebook before 2020 Election, Internal Report Shows," *MIT Technology Review*, September 16, 2021, https:// www.technologyreview.com/2021/09/16/1035851/facebook -troll-farms-report-us-2020-election/.

31. Daniel Tetteh Osabu-Kle, "The Politics of One-Sided Adjustment in Africa," *Journal of Black Studies* 30, no. 4 (2000): 515–33; Jason Hickel, "Apartheid in the World Bank and the IMF," *Al Jazeera*, November 26, 2020, https://www .aljazeera.com/opinions/2020/11/26/it-is-time-to-decolonise -the-world-bank-and-the-imf; Ngaire Woods, "Unelected Government: Making the IMF and the World Bank More Accountable," *Brookings* (blog), April 1, 2003 https://www .brookings.edu/articles/unelected-government-making-the -imf-and-the-world-bank-more-accountable/.

32. York W. Bradshaw and Jie Huang, "Intensifying Global Dependency: Foreign Debt, Structural Adjustment, and Third World Underdevelopment," *Sociological Quarterly* 32, no. 3 (1991): 321–42; Issa G. Shivji, "Samir Amin on Democracy and Fascism," *Agrarian South: Journal of Political Economy* 9, no. 1 (2020): 12–32.

33. Keston Perry, "Realising Climate Reparations: Towards a Global Climate Stabilization Fund and Resilience Fund Programme for Loss and Damage in Marginalised and Former Colonised Societies," *Social Science Research Network*, 2020.

34. Hickel, "Apartheid in the World Bank and the IMF."

35. Thea Riofrancos, *Resource Radicals: From Petro-nationalism to Post-extractivism in Ecuador* (Durham, NC: Duke University Press, 2020).

36. Shivji, "Samir Amin on Democracy and Fascism," 13.

37. Wolfgang Streeck, *How Will Capitalism End?: Essays on a Failing System* (London and New York: Verso, 2016), 20.

38. Stephen Ferguson, *Philosophy of African American Studies: Nothing Left of Blackness* (New York: Springer, 2015), 36.

39. Angela Yvonne Davis, "The Anti-slavery Movement and the Birth of Women's Rights," chapter 2 and "Class and Race in the Early Women's Rights Campaign," chapter 3 in *Women, Race, and Class* (New York: Vintage, 1983), 30–69.

40. This allegation is perhaps most famously made by Angela Davis in *Women, Race, and Class* but has been debated in the decades since. For an analysis tying Frazier's account to patriarchy, see Curwood; for a defense of Frazier, see Semmes. Davis, 14; Anastasia Curwood, "A FRESH LOOK AT E. FRANKLIN FRAZIER'S SEXUAL POLITICS IN THE NEGRO FAMILY IN THE UNITED STATES," *Du Bois Review: Social Science Research on Race* 5, no. 2 (2008): 325–37, https://doi.org/10.1017/S1742058X08080193; Clovis E. Semmes, "E. Franklin Frazier's Theory of the Black Family: Vindication and Sociological Insight," *J. Soc. & Soc. Welfare* 28, no. 2 (2001): 3.

41. Dawson, *Blacks in and out of the Left*.

42. Shannon Keating, "You Wanted Same-Sex Marriage? Now You Have Pete Buttigieg," *BuzzFeed News*, December 11, 2019, https://www.buzzfeednews.com/article/shannonkeating/pete-buttigieg-marriage-equality-lgbtq-gay-rights.

43. Barbara Smith, "Barbara Smith: Why I Left the Mainstream Queer Rights Movement," *New York Times*, June 19, 2019, https://www.nytimes.com/2019/06/19/us/barbara-smith-black-queer-rights.html.

Chapter 2: Reading the Room

1. Robert F. Durden, "In the Shadow of Slavery," *The Life of Carter G. Woodson: Father of African-American History* (New York: Enslow Publishers), 8–19.

2. Durden, *Life of Carter G. Woodson*, 8–19.

3. Durden, *Life of Carter G. Woodson*, 8–19; W. E. B. Du Bois, *Black Reconstruction in America: Toward a History of the Part Which Black Folk Played in the Attempt to Reconstruct Democracy in America, 1860–1880* (New York: Harcourt Brace, 1935); Guy Emerson Mount, "When Slaves Go on Strike: W.E.B. Du Bois's Black Reconstruction 80 Years Later," *Black Perspectives*, December 28, 2015,"https://www.aaihs.org/when-slaves-go-on-strike/.

4. Jarvis R. Givens, "Fugitive Pedagogy," in *Fugitive Pedagogy* (Cambridge, MA: Harvard University Press, 2021), 4.

5. Durden, "Student, Teacher, Traveler," chapter 3 in *Life of Carter G. Woodson*, 20–25.

6. Durden, *Life of Carter G. Woodson*, 20–25.

7. "Key Events in Black Higher Education," *Journal of Blacks in Higher Education* official website, n.d., https://www.jbhe.com/chronology/.

8. Durden, "Launching Negro History Week, chapter 6 in *Life of Carter G. Woodson*, 47–63; Robert F. Schwarzwalder, Jr., "Francis J. Grimke: Prophet of Racial Justice, Skeptic of American Power," excerpt (PhD diss., University of Aberdeen, 2021), accessed at Regent University Library Link (blog) on March 21, 2021, http://digitallibrary.regent.edu/wordpress/?p=3546.

9. Daryl Michael Scott, "The History of Black History Month," *Black Past*, January 14, 2010, https://www.blackpast.org/african-american-history/history-black-history-month/.

10. Givens, "Fugitive Pedagogy."

11. Scott, "The History of Black History Month."

12. This term is Herb Clark's; see his *Using Language* (Cambridge, UK: Cambridge University Press, 1996).

13. Robert Stalnaker, *Context* (Oxford: Oxford University Press, 1966), 68, 78.

14. Robert Stalnaker, "Common Ground," *Linguistics and Philoso-*

phy 25 (2002): 701–21; Stalnaker, *Context*.

15. See Olúfẹ́mi O. Táíwò, "The Empire Has No Clothes," *Disputatio* 51 (2018): 305–30.

16. Kelly F. Austin, "Degradation and Disease: Ecologically Unequal Exchanges Cultivate Emerging Pandemics," *World Development* 137 (2021): 105–63; J. L. Austin, "Performative Utterances," in *Philosophical Papers*, J. O. Urmson and G. J. Warnock eds. (Oxford: Clarendon Press, 1961); Rebecca Kukla and Mark Norris Lance, *"Yo!'and'Lo!": The Pragmatic Topography of the Space of Reasons* (Cambridge, MA: Harvard University Press, 2009).

17. David Lewis, "Scorekeeping in a Language Game," *Journal of Philosophical Logic* 8, no. 1 (1979).

18. Lewis, "Scorekeeping in a Language Game," 340.

19. Miranda Fricker, *Epistemic Injustice: Power and the Ethics of Knowing* (Oxford: Oxford University Press, 2007).

20. Tommie Shelby, "Ideology, Racism, and Critical Social Theory," *Philosophical Forum* 34, no. 2 (2003): 153–88.

21. Robin D. G. Kelley, "' We Are Not What We Seem': Rethinking Black Working-Class Opposition in the Jim Crow South" *Journal of American History* 80, no. 7 (1993): 75–112; James C. Scott, *Domination and the Arts of Resistance: Hidden Transcripts* (New Haven: Yale University Press, 1990).

22. Gerald Vizenor, *Shadow Distance: A Gerald Vizenor Reader* (Middletown, CT: Wesleyan University Press, 1994); Goran Gumze, "Capoeira: Influences on Depression, Aggression and Violence in Salvador," (Ph.D diss., University of Nova Gorica, 2014) 32.

23. Carol Hanisch, "The Personal Is Political," February 1969, carolhanisch.org.

24. Carter G. Woodson, *The Mis-Education of the Negro* (Middletown, CT: Tribeca Books, 2016), 4.

25. Woodson, "How We Drifted Away from the Truth," chapter

3 in *Mis-Education of the Negro*

26. C. Thi Nguyen, "Layers of Agency," chapter 3 and "Gamification and Value Capture," chapter 9 in *Games: Agency as Art* (Oxford: Oxford University Press, 2018), 52–73, 189–215.

27. Noam Scheiber, "How Uber Uses Psychological Tricks to Push Its Drivers' Buttons," *New York Times*, April 2, 2017, https://www.nytimes.com/interactive/2017/04/02 /technology/uber-drivers-psychological-tricks.html.

28. John Holden, "Big Companies Get Involved in Big Brother-Style Monitoring of Staff," *Irish Times*, August 18, 2014, https://www.irishtimes.com/business/big-companies-get -involved-in-big-brother-style-monitoring-of-staff-1.1898170; Sara Ashley O'Brien, "Workers at Amazon Brace for Another Grueling Week Spurred by Prime Day," *CNN*, June 21, 2021, https://www.cnn.com/2021/06/21/tech/workers -amazon-prime-day/index.html.

29. Nguyen, "Gamification and Value Capture," chapter 9 in *Games: Agency as Art*, 189–215.

30. Lewis, "Scorekeeping in a Language Game," 344–46.

31. Abigail Higgins and Olúfẹ́mi O. Táíwò, "Enforcing Eviction," *The Nation*, August 20, 2020, www.thenation.com /article/society/police-eviction-housing.

32. See Elizabeth Anderson, *Private Government: How Employers Rule Our Lives (and Why We Don't Talk about It)* (Princeton, NJ: Princeton University Press, 2017).

33. Arlie Russell Hochschild, *The Managed Heart: Commercialization of Human Feeling* (Berkeley: University of California Press, 1979).

34. Molly Jackman, "ALEC's Influence over Lawmaking in State Legislatures," *Brookings* (blog), December 6, 2013, www. brookings.edu/articles/alecs-influence-over-lawmaking -in-state-legislatures; Alexander C. Kaufman, "4 More States Propose Harsh New Penalties For Protesting Fossil Fuels,

HuffPost, February 20, 2021, www.huffpost.com/entry /fossil-fuel-protest_n_602c1ff6c5b6c95056f3f6af; Alexander C. Kaufman, "Yet Another State Quietly Moves to Criminalize Fossil Fuel Protests Amid Coronavirus," May 8, 2020, www.huffpost.com/entry/alabama-fossil-fuel-pipeline -protest-criminalize_n_5eb590b4c5b6197b8461d550.

35. George J. Stigler, "The Theory of Economic Regulation" *Bell Journal of Management Science* 2, no. 1 (1971): 3–21; Ernesto Dal Bó, "Regulatory Capture: A Review," *Oxford Review of Economic Policy* 22, no. 2 (2006): 203–225.

36. "Shell Sued in UK for 'Decades of Oil Spills' in Nigeria," *Al Jazeera*, November 22, 2016, www.aljazeera.com/news /2016/11/22/shell-sued-in-uk-for-decades-of-oil-spills-in -nigeria; Ike Okonta and Oronto Douglas, *Where Vultures Feast: Shell, Human Rights, and Oil in the Niger Delta* (London and New York: Verso, 2001).

37. Enegide Chinedu and Chukwuma Kelechukwu Chukwuemeka, "Oil Spillage and Heavy Metals Toxicity Risk in the Niger Delta, Nigeria"; Noah, A.O., Adhikari, P., Ogundele, B.O. and Yazdifar, H. (2021), "Corporate environmental accountability in Nigeria: an example of regulatory failure and regulatory capture," *Journal of Accounting in Emerging Economies* 11, no. 1, https://doi.org/10.1108/JAEE-02-2019 -0038, 70–93; Bukola Adebayo, "Major New Inquiry into Oil Spills in Niger Delta Launched," CNN, March 26, 2019, https://www.cnn.com/2019/03/26/africa/nigeria-oil-spill-in quiry-intl/index.html.

38. Davide Calenda and Albert Meijer, "Political Individualization: New Media as an Escape from Family Control over Political Behavior," *Information, Communication & Society* 14, no. 5 (2011): 660–83.

39. Woodson, *Mis-Education of the Negro*, 20–21.

40. Saray Ayala, "Speech Affordances: A Structural Take on How

Much We Can Do with Our Words," *European Journal of Philosophy* 24, no. 4 (2016): 879–91; Táíwò, "Empire Has No Clothes."

41. Ayala, "Speech Affordances"; Kristie Dotson, "Conceptualizing Epistemic Oppression," *Social Epistemology*, 2014.

42. See Kukla and Lance, *"Yo!'and'Lo!"*

Chapter 3: Being in the Room

An earlier version of this essay appeared as "Being-in-the-Room Privilege: Elite Capture and Epistemic Difference," *The Philosopher* vol. 108, no. 4, https://www.thephilosopher1923.org/essay-taiwo.

1. Walter Rodney, *How Europe Underdeveloped Africa* (London and Dar Es Salaam: Bogle-L'Ouverture Publications, 1972).

2. Amílcar Cabral, *Return to the Source: Selected Speeches of Amílcar Cabral* (New York: Monthly Review Press, 1973), 51.

3. George E. Brooks, "Cabo Verde: Gulag of the South Atlantic: Racism, Fishing Prohibitions, and Famines," *History in Africa* 33 (2006): 101, https://doi.org/10.1353/hia.2006.0008.

4. Lilica Boal, "Mulheres de Abril: Testemunho de Lilica Boal," *Esquerda*, November 24, 2019, https://www.esquerda.net/artigo/mulheres-de-abril-testemunho-de-lilica-boal/64575.

5. Brooks, "Cabo Verde," 134.

6. Brooks, "Cabo Verde," 107, 111.

7. Brooks, "Cabo Verde," 107.

8. Brooks, "Cabo Verde," 107–11.

9. Alexander Keese, "Managing the Prospect of Famine: Cape Verdean Officials, Subsistence Emergencies, and the Change of Elite Attitudes During Portugal's Late Colonial Phase, 1939–1961," *Itinerario* 36, no. 1 (2012): 51.

10. Boal, "Mulheres de Abril."

11. Boal, "Mulheres de Abril."

12. Boal, "Mulheres de Abril."

13. Boal, "Mulheres de Abril."

14. Boal, "Mulheres de Abril."

15. Boal, "Mulheres de Abril."

16. Boal, "Mulheres de Abril"; António Tomás, *Amílcar Cabral: The Life of a Reluctant Nationalist* (London: Hurst & Co., 2021), 127–28.

17. World Health Organization, "1 in 3 People Globally Do Not Have Access to Safe Drinking Water – UNICEF, WHO," news release, June 18, 2021, https://www.who.int/news/item /18-06-2019-1-in-3-people-globally-do-not-have-access-to -safe-drinking-water-unicef-who; United Nations, "Affordable Housing Key for Development and Social Equality, UN Says on World Habitat Day," October 2, 2017, https://news. un.org/en/story/2017/10/567552-affordable-housing-key -development-and-social-equality-un-says-world-habitat.

18. Briana Toole, "Demarginalizing Standpoint Epistemology," *Episteme* 1 (2020): 19; Briana Toole, "From Standpoint Epistemology to Epistemic Oppression," *Hypatia* 34, no. 4 (2019): 598–618; Internet Encyclopedia of Philosophy, "Feminist Standpoint Theory," *Internet Encyclopedia of Philosophy*, https://iep.utm.edu/fem-stan/.

19. Liam Kofi Bright, "Empiricism Is a Standpoint Epistemology," *The Sooty Empiric* (blog), June 2018, https://sootyempiric .blogspot.com/2018/06/empiricism-is-standpoint -epistemology.html.

20. Priscilla Frank, "Touching Animation Recounts Story of Obama's 'Fired Up, Ready To Go' Chant," *HuffPost*, January 19, 2017, https://www.huffpost.com/entry/animated -film-obama-fired-up_n_5880ebd4e4b0e3a73567767e; Byron Tau, "The Story of 'Fired up! Ready to Go,'" *Politico*, April 4, 2012, https://www.politico.com/blogs/politico44/2012/04 /the-story-of-fired-up-ready-to-go-119612; Jeff Zeleny and Michael M. Grynbaum, "Obama Wins South Carolina Pri-

mary," *New York Times*, January 26, 2008, https://www
.nytimes.com/2008/01/26/us/politics/26cnd-carolina.html.

21. "Fired Up? Ready to Go?," White House official website, September 13, 2009, available at https://obamawhitehouse.archives
.gov/blog/2009/09/13/fired-ready-go.

22. Jo Freeman, "The Tyranny of Stucturelessness," Jo Freeman official website, https://www.jofreeman.com/joreen/tyranny.htm.

23. Freeman, "Tyranny of Stucturelessness."

24. Stephen Rohde, "The United States—A Model for the Nazis," *Los Angeles Review of Books*, September 3, 2017, https://lareviewofbooks.org/article/the-united-states-a-model-for
-the-nazis/; James Q. Whitman, *Hitler's American Model: The United States and the Making of Nazi Race Law* (Princeton, NJ: Princeton University Press, 2017).

25. "Forty Percent of Nigerians Live below the Poverty Line: Report," *Al Jazeera*, May 4, 2020, https://www.aljazeera.com
/economy/2020/5/4/forty-percent-of-nigerians-live-below
-the-poverty-line-report; "The Most Successful Ethnic Group in the U.S. May Surprise You," *OZY*, January 6, 2018, https://www.ozy.com/around-the-world/the-most-successful
-ethnic-group-in-the-u-s-may-surprise-you/86885/; Leslie Casimir, "Data Show Nigerians the Most Educated in the U.S.," *Chron*, May 20, 2008, https://www.chron.com/news
/article/Data-show-Nigerians-the-most-educated-in-the
-U-S-1600808.php.

26. See Olúfémi O. Táíwò, "Being-in-the-Room Privilege: Elite Capture and Epistemic Deference," *The Philosopher* 108, no. 4 (2020).

27. Robert K Merton, "The Matthew Effect in Science: The Reward and Communication Systems of Science Are Considered," *Science* 159, no. 3810 (1968): 56–63; Paul D Allison, J Scott Long, and Tad K Krauze, "Cumulative Advantage and Inequality in Science," *American Sociological Review*, 1982, 615–25; Robert J

Sampson and John H Laub, "A Life-Course Theory of Cumulative Disadvantage and the Stability of Delinquency," *Developmental Theories of Crime and Delinquency* 7 (1997): 133–61.

28. Cabral, "National Liberation and Culture," Transition, no. 45 (1974): 12–17.

29. Cabral, "National Liberation and Culture."

Chapter 4: Building a New House

1. Amílcar Cabral, *Análise de Alguns Tipos de Resistência, Edição Do PAIGC* (Bolama: Guiné-Bissau Imprensa Nacional, 1979), my translation, available at http://www.cd25a.uc.pt/media /pdf/Biblioteca%20digital/Nreg%200715_%20Amilcar%20 Cabral_Analise%20se%20alguns%20tipos%20de%20 resistencia.pdf.

2. Paulo Freire, *Pedagogy of the Oppressed: 30th Anniversary*, M. B. Ramos, trans. (New York: Continuum, 1970), 30.

3. Paulo Freire, *Letters to Cristina* (London: Routledge, 2016), 21.

4. Freire, *Letters to Cristina*, 21.

5. Freire, *Pedagogy of the Oppressed*, 35; Anthony W. Pereira, "The US Role in the 1964 Coup in Brazil: A Reassessment," *Bulletin of Latin American Research* 37, no. 1 (2018): 5–17.

6. Freire, chapter 2 in *Pedagogy of the Oppressed*, 71–86.

7. Freire, *Pedagogy of the Oppressed*, 74–76.

8. Francisco J. Beltrán Tapia et al., "A Brief History of the Reconquista (718–1492 AD): Conquest, Repopulation and Land Distribution," *Documentos de Trabajo de la Sociedad Española de Historia Agraria*, 2004.

9. Peter Karibe Mendy, *Amílcar Cabral: A Nationalist and Pan-Africanist Revolutionary* (Athens: Ohio University Press, 2019), 24–28, 37.

10. Peter Karibe Mendy, "Portugal's Civilizing Mission in

Colonial Guinea-Bissau: Rhetoric and Reality," *International Journal of African Historical Studies* 36, no. 1 (2003): 35–58.

11. Mendy, *Amílcar Cabral*, 24–28.
12. Mendy, *Amílcar Cabral*, 29.
13. Mendy, *Amílcar Cabral*, 33.
14. Luís Reis Torgal, "Estado, Ideologia e História de Portugal," *Revista de História* 8 (1988): 345–55.
15. Stephanie Urdang, "Fighting Two Colonialisms: The Women's Struggle in Guinea-Bissau," *African Studies Review* 18, no. 3 (1975): 29.
16. Sónia Vaz Borges, *Militant Education, Liberation Struggle, Consciousness: The PAIGC Education in Guinea-Bissau 1963–1978* (Berlin: Peter Lang, 2019).
17. Vaz Borges, "The PAIGC's Freedom Fighter. The Process of Becoming Conscious and a Militant (1940's-1972)," *Militant Education*, 23–53.
18. Vaz Borges, *Militant Education*, 25.
19. Vaz Borges, *Militant Education*, 119.
20. Vaz Borges, *Militant Education*, 126.
21. Vaz Borges, "Building and Organizing Educational Structures in Guinea Bissau (1963-1972)," *Militant Education*, 53–98.
22. R. A. Akindele, "Africa and the Great Powers, with Particular Reference to the United States, the Soviet Union and China," *Africa Spectrum*, 1985, 125–51; Julião Soares Sousa, "Amílcar Cabral, the PAIGC and the Relations with China at the Time of the Sino-Soviet Split and of Anti-colonialism: Discourses and Praxis," *International History Review* 42, no. 6 (2020): 1274–96; Catarina Laranjeiro, "The Cuban Revolution and the Liberation Struggle in Guinea-Bissau: Images, Imaginings, Expectations and Experiences," *International History Review* 42, no. 6 (2020): 1319–38.
23. Suzanne Lipinska, "Two Weeks With the Guinea-Bissau Liberation Army," in *Cinéma Chez Les Balantes*, trans. Caroline

Higgitt (Ghent: KIOSK, 2014), 40.

24. Vaz Borges, *Militant Education*, 125; Lilica Boal, "Mulheres de Abril: Testemunho de Lilica Boal," *Esquerda*, November 24, 2019, https://www.esquerda.net/artigo/mulheres-de-abril-testemunho-de-lilica-boal/64575.

25. Vaz Borges, *Militant Education*, 66.

26. Vaz Borges, *Militant Education*, 62–65.

27. Urdang, "Fighting Two Colonialisms," 30.

28. Urdang, "Fighting Two Colonialisms," 30.

29. Lipinska, "Two Weeks with the Guinea-Bissau Liberation Army," 9.

30. Vaz Borges, *Militant Education*, 163.

31. Vaz Borges, *Militant Education*, 164–66.

32. Marina Padrão Temudo and Manuel Bivar Abrantes, "Changing Policies, Shifting Livelihoods: The Fate of Agriculture in Guinea-Bissau," *Journal of Agrarian Change* 13, no. 4 (2013): 575.

33. António Tomás, *Amílcar Cabral: The Life of a Reluctant Nationalist* (London: Hurst & Co., 2021), 127.

34. Maria do Carmo Rebouças da Cruz and Ferreira dos Santos, "A Recolonização de Guiné-Bissau Por Meio Das Representações Negativas Realizadas Pelos Organismos Internacionais de Desenvolvimento: De 'Estado Frágil' a 'Narco-Estado,'" *Desenvolvimento Em Questão* 17, no. 47 (2019): 156–78; Tomás, *Amílcar Cabral.*

35. Thomas C. Bruneau, "The Guinea-Bissau Case" in *Security Forces in African States*, Paula Shmella and Nicholas Tomb, ed (Amherst, NY: Cambria Press, 2017).

36. Julião Soares Sousa, "Prefácio," in *Por Uma Reinvenção Da Governabilidade e Do Equilíbrio de Poder Na Guiné-Bissau: Diálogos e Olhares Cruzado a Partir Da Diáspora* (Middletown, CT: independently published, 2014), 3–4.

37. Mark Shaw, "Drug Trafficking in Guinea-Bissau, 1998–2014: The Evolution of an Elite Protection Network," *Journal of*

Modern African Studies 53, no. 3 (2015): 339–64; Emmanuel Uzuegbu-Wilson, "A Critical Review of Evolutionary Trends of Drug Trafficking in Guinea-Bissau," *Social Science Research Network*, 2019.

38. "Is Cape Verde Doomed to Become a Narco-State?," *ENACT Africa*, June 4, 2019, https://enactafrica.org/enact-observer/is-cape-verde-doomed-to-become-a-narco-state; Colin Freeman, "The Cocaine Highway: On the Front Line of Europe's Drug War," *Telegraph*, November 3, 2019, https://www.telegraph.co.uk/news/drug-trafficking-in-cape-verde/.

39. Ashley Neese Bybee, *Narco State or Failed State? Narcotics and Politics in Guinea-Bissau* (Fairfax, VA: George Mason University Press, 2011); Sonia Pires, "Guinea-Bissau Immigrant Transnationalism in Portugal: A Substitute for a Failed State?," *African and Black Diaspora: An International Journal* 6, no. 2 (2013): 145–73.

40. "Guinea-Bissau," UNESCO, November 27, 2016, http://uis.unesco.org/en/country/gw; Bruneau, "The Guinea-Bissau Case."

41. African Development Bank, "Cape Verde: A Success Story," November 2012, https://www.afdb.org/sites/default/files/documents/projects-and-operations/cape_verde_-_a_success_story.pdf.

42. Peter Meyns, "Cape Verde: An African Exception," *Journal of Democracy* 13, no. 3 (2002): 153–65; Bruce Baker, "Cape Verde: The Most Democratic Nation in Africa?," *Journal of Modern African Studies*, 2006, 493–511.

43. Boal, "Mulheres de Abril."

44. António Tomás, *Amílcar Cabral: The Life of a Reluctant Nationalist* (London: Hurst & Co., 2021), 137; Lipinska, "Two Weeks With the Guinea-Bissau Liberation Army," 2.

45. Lipinska, "Two Weeks With the Guinea-Bissau Liberation Army," 17.

46. Amílcar Cabral and Richard Handyside, "Message to the People of Portugal" (Khartoum, 1969), available at https://www.marxists.org/subject/africa/cabral/1969/mpp.htm.

47. Lipinska, "Two Weeks With the Guinea-Bissau Liberation Army," 42.

48. Mendy, *Amílcar Cabral*, 64–65.

49. Reiland Rabaka, "Cabral's Critical Theory of Colonialism, Neocolonialism, and Imperialism," chapter 3 in *Concepts of Cabralism: Amilcar Cabral and Africana Critical Theory* (Lexington Books, 2014), 151–82.

50. José Javier Olivas Osuna, "The Deep Roots of the Carnation Revolution: 150 Years of Military Interventionism in Portugal," *Portuguese Journal of Social Science* 13, no. 2 (2014): 224.

51. António Tomás, "Introduction: Decolonising the 'Undecolonisable'? Portugal and the Independence of Lusophone Africa," *Social Dynamics* 42, no. 1 (January 2, 2016): 3, https://doi.org/10.1080/02533952.2016.1164956.

52. Osuna, "Deep Roots of the Carnation Revolution," 225.

53. Raquel Varela, "Today, We Celebrate the Carnation Revolution," interview by David Broder, *Jacobin*, April 25, 2019, https://jacobinmag.com/2019/04/portugal-carnation-revolution-national-liberation-april.

54. Tomás, "Decolonising the 'Undecolonisable'?"

55. Noam Chomsky, *Media Control: The Spectacular Achievements of Propaganda*, 2nd ed. (New York: Seven Stories Press, 2002), 20.

56. "Economic Justice," The Movement for Black Lives, https://policy.m4bl.org/.

57. Fantu Cheru, "Democracy and People Power in Africa: Still Searching for the 'Political Kingdom,'" *Third World Quarterly* 33, no. 2 (2012): 265–91; Jeffrey Williams, "The Pedagogy of Debt," *College Literature* 33, no. 4 (2006): 155–69.

58. Donella H. Meadows, *Thinking in Systems: A Primer* (Hartford, VT: Chelsea Green Publishing, 2008), 80.

59. Merrit Kennedy, "Lead-Laced Water In Flint: A Step-by-Step Look at the Makings of a Crisis," NPR, April 20, 2016, https://www.npr.org/sections/thetwo-way/2016/04/20/465545378/lead-laced-water-in-flint-a-step-by-step-look-at-the-makings-of-a-crisis.

60. Olúfẹ́mi O. Táíwò and Liam Kofi Bright, "A Response to Michael Walzer," *Dissent Magazine* (blog), https://www.dissentmagazine.org/online_articles/a-response-to-michael-walzer; Robin D. G. Kelley, "What Did Cedric Robinson Mean by Racial Capitalism?," *Boston Review*, January 12, 2017, https://bostonreview.net/race/robin-d-g-kelley-what-did-cedric-robinson-mean-racial-capitalism; Yousuf Al-Bulushi, "Thinking Racial Capitalism and Black Radicalism from Africa: An Intellectual Geography of Cedric Robinson's World-System," *Geoforum*, January 31, 2020, https://doi.org/10.1016/j.geoforum.2020.01.018.

61. Ole F. Norheim et al., "Difficult Trade-Offs in Response to COVID-19: The Case for Open and Inclusive Decision Making," *Nature Medicine* 27, no. 1 (January 1, 2021): 10–13, https://doi.org/10.1038/s41591-020-01204-6; Kyle Powys Whyte and Robert P. Crease, "Trust, Expertise, and the Philosophy of Science," *Synthese* 177, no. 3 (2010): 411–25; Gabriele Contessa, "It Takes a Village to Trust Science: Towards a (Thoroughly) Social Approach to Social Trust in Science" (unpublished research paper), 2021.

62. Micah Herskind, "Some Reflections on Prison Abolition after #MUMI," Medium, September 23, 2020, https://micahherskind.medium.com/some-reflections-on-prison-abolition-after-mumi-5197a4c3cf98.

63. Firoze Manji, "Amilcar Cabral and Ken Saro-Wiwa: Their Commonalities on Culture and the Struggle for Freedom," *Ukombozi Review* (blog), September 6, 2020, https://ukombozireview.com/blog/amilcar-cabral-and-ken-saro

-wiwa-their-commonalities-on-culture-and-the-struggle
-for-freedom/.

64. Caroline Shenaz Hossein, *The Black Social Economy in
the Americas: Exploring Diverse Community-Based Markets* (Springer, 2017); Caroline Shenaz Hossein, "Daring
to Conceptualize the Black Social Economy," in *The Black
Social Economy in the Americas* (Springer, 2018), 1–13; Jessica
Gordon Nembhard, *Collective Courage: A History of African
American Cooperative Economic Thought and Practice* (University Park: Penn State Press, 2014).

65. Joe William Trotter Jr., *Workers on Arrival: Black Labor in the
Making of America* (Berkeley: University of California Press,
2019); Olúfẹ́mi O. Táíwò and Dylan Plummer, "Just Transition: Learning From the Tactics of Past Labor Movements,"
The Trouble, October 12, 2020, https://www.the-trouble.com
/content/2020/10/12/just-transition-learning-from-the
-tactics-of-past-labor-movements.

66. Urdang, "Fighting Two Colonialisms."

67. Anthony Faiola, "Egypt's Labor Movement Blooms in Arab
Spring," *Washington Post*, September 25, 2011, https://www
.washingtonpost.com/world/middle-east/egypts-labor
-movement-blooms-in-arab-spring/2011/09/25/gIQAj6AfwK
_story.html; "The Arab Spring and Independent Trade
Unions: High Hopes and New Challenges—ITUC Survey of
Violations of Trade Union Rights," Survey of Violations of
Trade Union Rights, https://survey.ituc-csi.org/The
-Arab-Spring-and-independent.html?lang=en; Urdang,
"Fighting Two Colonialisms."

68. Dominika V. Polanska, Hannes Rolf, and Scott Springfeldt,
"Tenants Organizing: Precarization and Resistance," Radical
Housing Journal 3, no. 1 (2021): 121–29.

69. Jim Shultz, "The Cochabamba Water Revolt and Its Aftermath," in *Dignity and Defiance* (Berkeley: University of Cal-

ifornia Press, 2009), 9–44; Debt Collective, *Can't Pay, Won't Pay: The Case for Economic Disobedience and Debt Abolition* (Chicago: Haymarket Books, 2020).

70. Amilcar Cabral, "National Liberation and Culture" in *Return to the Source* (New York: Africa Information Service, 1973), 39–57.

71. Cabral, "National Liberation and Culture," 40–41, 43.

72. Cabral, "National Liberation and Culture," 51–52.

Chapter 5: The Point Is to Change It

1. Karl Marx, "Theses on Feuerbach," *Marx-Engels Selected Works*, vol. 1 (Moscow: Progress Publishers, 1969), 13–15.

2. Andaiye, "The Contemporary Caribbean Struggle," in *The Point Is to Change the World: Selected Writings of Andaiye*, Alissa Trotz, ed. (London: Pluto Press, 2020).

3. Clem Seecharan, "Foreword," in Andaiye, *The Point Is to Change the World*.

4. Andaiye, "Contemporary Caribbean Struggle."

5. Global Facility for Disaster Reduction and Recovery, "Stories of Impact: Communicating Flood Risk Along Guyana's Coast - Guyana." ReliefWeb, November 3, 2016, https://reliefweb.int /report/guyana/stories-impact-communicating-flood-risk -along-guyana-s-coast.

6. Ruth Wilson Gilmore, *Golden Gulag: Prisons, Surplus, Crisis, and Opposition in Globalizing California* (Berkeley: University of California Press, 2007), 176–78.

7. Keeanga-Yamahtta Taylor, *How We Get Free: Black Feminism and the Combahee River Collective* (Chicago: Haymarket Books, 2017), 117.

8. Briana Toole, "From Standpoint Epistemology to Epistemic Oppression," *Hypatia* 34, no. 4 (2019): 598–618; Briana Toole,

"Demarginalizing Standpoint Epistemology," *Episteme* 1 (2020): 19.

9. Agnes Callard, "The Philosophy of Anger," *Boston Review*, April 16, 2020, https://bostonreview.net/forum/agnes -callard-philosophy-anger.

10. Nick Estes (@nickwestes), Twitter, September 4, 2020, 4:40 pm, https://twitter.com/nickwestes/status /1301998637740851201.

11. Jane Howard, "Doom and Glory of Knowing Who You Are," *Life*, May 24, 1963.

Index

About the Author

Olúfẹ́mi O. Táíwò is assistant professor of philosophy at Georgetown University. He received his PhD in philosophy at the University of California, Los Angeles. He has published in academic journals ranging from *Public Affairs Quarterly*, *One Earth*, *Philosophical Papers*, and the American Philosophical Association newsletter *Philosophy and the Black Experience*.

Táíwò's theoretical work draws liberally from the Black radical tradition, anti-colonial thought, German transcendental philosophy, contemporary philosophy of language, contemporary social science, and histories of activism and activist thinkers.

His public philosophy, including articles exploring intersections of climate justice and colonialism, has been featured in *The Nation*, *Boston Review*, *Dissent*, *The Appeal*, *Slate*, *Al Jazeera*, the *New Republic*, *Aeon*, and *Foreign Policy*.

He is the author of the book *Reconsidering Reparations*, published by Oxford University Press.

About Haymarket Books

Haymarket Books is a radical, independent, nonprofit book publisher based in Chicago.

Our mission is to publish books that contribute to struggles for social and economic justice. We strive to make our books a vibrant and organic part of social movements and the education and development of a critical, engaged, international left.

We take inspiration and courage from our namesakes, the Haymarket martyrs, who gave their lives fighting for a better world. Their 1886 struggle for the eight-hour day—which gave us May Day, the international workers' holiday—reminds workers around the world that ordinary people can organize and struggle for their own liberation. These struggles continue today across the globe—struggles against oppression, exploitation, poverty, and war.

Since our founding in 2001, Haymarket Books has published more than five hundred titles. Radically independent, we seek to drive a wedge into the risk-averse world of corporate book publishing. Our authors include Noam Chomsky, Arundhati Roy, Rebecca Solnit, Angela Y. Davis, Howard Zinn, Amy Goodman, Wallace Shawn, Mike Davis, Winona LaDuke, Ilan Pappé, Richard Wolff, Dave Zirin, Keeanga-Yamahtta Taylor, Nick Turse, Dahr Jamail, David Barsamian, Elizabeth Laird, Amira Hass, Mark Steel, Avi Lewis, Naomi Klein, and Neil Davidson. We are also the trade publishers of the acclaimed Historical Materialism Book Series and of Dispatch Books.

Also Available
from Haymarket Books

Abolition. Feminism. Now. by Angela Y. Davis, Gina Dent, Erica R. Meiners, and Beth E. Richie

Angela Davis: An Autobiography by Angela Y. Davis

Assata Taught Me: State Violence, Racial Capitalism, and the Movement for Black Lives by Donna Murch

Border and Rule: Global Migration, Capitalism, and the Rise of Racist Nationalism by Harsha Walia. afterword by Nick Estes, foreword by Robin D.G. Kelley

From #BlackLivesMatter to Black Liberation by Keeanga-Yamahtta Taylor, foreword by Angela Y. Davis

Speaking Out of Place: Getting Our Political Voices Back by David Palumbo-Liu

We Do This 'Til We Free Us: Abolitionist Organizing and Transforming Justice by Mariame Kaba, edited by Tamara K. Nopper, foreword by Naomi Murakawa

We Still Here: Pandemic, Policing, Protest, and Possibility by Marc Lamont Hill, edited by Frank Barat, foreword by Keeanga-Yamahtta Taylor

CPSIA information can be obtained
at www.ICGtesting.com
Printed in the USA
BVHW051140170123
656433BV00003B/184